The Bible of Cognitive Behavioral Therapy Made Simple:

2 books in 1 :

Retrain Your Brain Using CBT to Overcome Anxiety, Fears, Phobias, Depression and Panic Disorder - Declutter Your Mind and Be Happy

Daniel Anderson

COGNITIVE BEHAVIORAL THERAPY MADE SIMPLE

By

Daniel Anderson

TABLE OF CONTENTS

INTRODUCTION.. 6

CHAPTER ONE: COGNITIVE BEHAVIORAL
    THERAPY.. 22

CHAPTER TWO: EXERCISES DESIGNED TO
    DEAL WITH ANXIETY.................................37

CHAPTER THREE: FEAR IN THE BRAIN................56

CHAPTER FOUR: SUREFIRE WAYS TO GET RID
    OF BAD HABITS..64

CHAPTER FIVE: STRONGER FOR THE
    EXPERIENCE...85

CHAPTER SIX: PRACTICING MINDFULNESS
    MEDIATION...91

CHAPTER SEVEN: RECOVERY GUIDE TO
    ANXIETY DISORDERS........................... 133

INTRODUCTION

We must have all experienced our hearts pounding very fast before a major job interview or when we are asked to make a speech before important personalities. We worry over family and financial problems or feel jittery at the prospect of meeting a date for the first time. If your worries and fears are preventing you from living your life in a normal way, you may very well be suffering from an anxiety disorder. Here we want to show you simple techniques you can use to prevent and overcome anxiety. These techniques have been reported as indeed panic attacks and anxiety cures.

You are free to take the techniques seriously and stop swallowing dangerous panic attacks medication in order to completely eliminate panic attacks from your life. I was once an anxiety and panic attacks sufferer. I missed several important job interviews because of this problem until I was able to find a permanent cure using the One Move technique. Before I used the One Move technique to cure my panic attacks and anxiety, these were the techniques - cognitive behavioral therapy and graded exposure therapy - that helped me overcome anxiety and panic attacks.

Cognitive behavioral therapy and graded exposure therapy are the two effective anxiety and panic attacks treatment techniques. The two techniques are actually behavioral therapy and they focus on behavioral modifications rather than on underlying psychological problems of the past. The two techniq ues took me between 5 and 20 weekly sessions.

Cognitive behavior therapy - focuses on your thoughts and behavior modifications. When used in panic attacks anxiety cures, cognitive behavioral therapy helped me identify and challenge the negative thinking patterns and irrational beliefs that are fueling my anxiety and panic attacks.

Graded exposure therapy - This technique helped me to confront my fears in a safe and controlled manner. Through repeated and graded exposures to the feared situations, I was able to acquire a greater sense of control of myself. As I was being made to face my fears without being harmed, my anxiety and panic attacks gradually disappeared.

I believe strongly that these techniques are the best approach to treating and eliminating the twin problems of anxiety and panic attacks. Even the medical world now agrees that the best treatment for anxiety disorder is through behavioral therapy. The One Move technique is an advanced from of behavioral therapy which I used to completely cure all my symptoms. This is a heart-warming news to all sufferers. Your panic attacks and anxiety can be cured without costly and dangerous antidepressant medications.

Feel confident and beautiful once more. Experience for yourself the immediate and fast cure for panic attacks and anxiety with the One Move technique.

How do you overcome Anxiety?

Steps to Overcoming Anxiety

With the aid of the lists below, you can successfully overcome anxiety;

Overcoming anxiety after it's developed into a major difficulty in your life can often be confusing and upsetting. However, anxiety disorders are very treatable problems.

This is a consumer guide for people who seek anxiety relief, but don't know how to get there. However, I suggest that everyone who seeks relief from chronic anxiety should review these steps, and complete any which you haven't yet done.

Step One:

Learn a little about anxiety disorders

Understanding how anxiety "works" is one of the keys to overcoming anxiety. Read my description of the different anxiety disorders and compare your experience with those descriptions.

Use the book to learn more about overcoming anxiety disorders. The purpose here is not to self-diagnose yourself - please consult a licensed clinician for a diagnosis - but to inform yourself as much as possible before you consult a clinician so that you can evaluate what a clinician tells you, be an informed consumer, and find effective methods for overcoming anxiety.

The internet is full of anxiety scams, so be wary! When something sounds too good to be true, it probably is.

It's common to experience some depression along with an anxiety disorder, and this is often a source of confusion to people. If this sounds relevant to you, read a little bit about depression.

Step Two:

Consult with your primary physician

A consultation with your physician is a must if you suspect you have panic attacks or generalized anxiety.

These symptoms can be caused by a variety of physiological disorders, and you should rule them out as part of the diagnostic process. You should certainly have one complete physical after the onset of these symptoms.

The other anxiety disorders don't generally require a physical, because there isn't any reason to think that they are caused by another physical ailment. However, you might still want to consult your physician, especially if you have a long history with that person. You might want his/her opinion about your situation; you might want a referral; or you might want to find out about possible medications you could use.

Be aware, however, that most physicians, because they specialize in various aspects of physical health, have very little training in the area of anxiety disorders. What training they do have, with respect to overcoming anxiety, is usually limited to medications. They may often be surprisingly unaware of cognitive behavioral treatment for anxiety disorders, even though it is generally regarded as the treatment of choice. When it comes time to seek professional help for overcoming anxiety disorders, you will probably need to go elsewhere.

If you don't have panic attacks or generalized anxiety, and have no other reason to consult your physician about overcoming anxiety, then skip ahead to Step Three.

Before you call for an appointment, make some written notes of what you want to discuss with your physician. The doctor's staff will probably ask you why you want an appointment; tell them that you've been having some problems and summarize them, briefly.

Many people have a fear of doctors, and have trouble making an appointment. This is a phobia, and will generally respond to the same CBT approach, once you decide that a visit to the doctor, however anxiety provoking, is in your best interest.

What to Expect from Your Physician

Your physician should listen to your symptoms, review your history, ask questions, and offer feedback and recommendations for overcoming anxiety. Since most physicians are trained principally in physical health and medicine, there is no reason to expect him/her to be an expert in anxiety disorders. However, your physician should take your complaints seriously, evaluate them, and offer suggestions for finding additional help.

If you are having panic attacks and have never been tested for thyroid malfunction, for instance, you should receive such a test, because thyroid problems can sometimes cause a person to have panic-like symptoms. If your symptoms resemble those associated with mitral valve prolapse, you should probably have an echocardiogram to evaluate that possibility. There are numerous physical conditions which can produce panic symptoms, and your physician should evaluate you for those possibilities if that has never been done before.

However, if you have had those tests before, and your doctor assured you that you were in good health, do not push for continual retesting! Many people do this because they hate the idea that they may have an anxiety disorder, and instead hope to find a physical problem. You can waste lots of time and money this way.

One set of tests is generally enough. If you need a second opinion for a particular reason, then get one. If you get more than two sets of tests, seriously consider the possibility that you are getting diverted from your task of overcoming anxiety!

Let's suppose that you've had a good consultation with your physician, the appropriate tests have ruled out any physical ailments which could be causing your symptoms, and you want to get professional help with overcoming anxiety. Now you're ready for step three.

Step Three:

Learn about the available treatments

There are basically two kinds of treatment which clinical research has shown to be effective in overcoming anxiety disorders: cognitive behavioral treatment (CBT) and certain forms of medication. Other forms of psychotherapy are often helpful in resolving some of the issues associated with anxiety disorders, but are generally not regarded as capable of resolving the primary problem. Which form of treatment should you choose?

My view is that most people with anxiety disorders are best served by trying a cognitive behavioral treatment first, and seeing what kind of results you get from that. You can always try medication later, if the CBT doesn't provide all the results you seek.

There are three principal reasons to try CBT first. First, unlike medication, CBT has no side effects. Second, the use of medications tends to lead a person to believe that he or she is now "protected" from anxiety disorders, and the sense of being protected often leads an anxiety sufferer to feel more vulnerable in the long run. Third, the results you get from CBT treatment will generally be much more long lasting than those you get from medications. Results from medication treatments tend to fade after the medications are withdrawn.

Some patients will need medication in addition to CBT, and some will not, depending on the severity of their condition and their particular diagnosis. Medication is nothing to be avoided if it seems necessary. However, I do believe it's true that in our culture, medications are overprescribed for these problems. This can be avoided if you start with CBT first.

The Anxiety Disorders Association of America website includes an overview of medications used to treat anxiety disorders

There are new forms of CBT in development, often labeled as "Third Wave" therapies. One in particular, Acceptance and Commitment Therapy (ACT) is quite useful in the treatment of Panic Disorder and other anxiety disorders. In my work, I blend methods from both traditional CBT and ACT, and find them both very useful in overcoming anxiety disorders.

Do I Need "Treatment" at All?

You may be wondering if you really need to see a professional, or if you can't just solve this problem on your own. In general, the more difficulty you are having, the more you may need professional help, but only you can decide how urgent your need is. Certainly there are many good sources of self help information you can use in overcoming anxiety disorders. If you choose to try anxiety self help, I suggest you follow a few guidelines.

* Get a "buddy", a coach, or a support person, with whom you can discuss your efforts on a regular basis. They don't have to be an expert. A major benefit is that, by telling someone of your efforts, you will find it easier to monitor your progress and hold yourself accountable. It's easy to forget about all your good intentions when you keep them to yourself.

* Follow an organized plan. Find a good self help book which pertains to your problem, and make that the basis of your work. If you have panic attacks and like the approach you find on this website, then try my Panic Attacks Workbook. If your problem is more about chronic worry, take a look at my book for chronic worriers, The Worry Trick.

* Evaluate your progress at regular intervals, at least monthly. After six months, re-evaluate your progress. If you're satisfied you're making reasonable progress toward overcoming anxiety, continue on course. If you're not, consider seeking professional help at that time.

What about Group Treatment for overcoming anxiety?

Among the advantages of group treatment for overcoming anxiety are lower cost and the opportunity to share experiences with others who can relate to your situation. This can be particularly important for people who feel especially ashamed and imagine that they are one of a very few who suffer in this way.

I don't really think there are any disadvantages to a well run group treatment, although many people shy away from it because they believe they would pick up more fears from hearing other people's problems. In my experience in running groups, this has not been a problem and, while people are usually quite nervous before the first meeting, their anxiety is usually much lower by the end of the meeting.

Group treatments are often not available, so consider yourself fortunate if they are offered in your area. Your own personal preference is probably the most important deciding factor in the choice between group and individual treatment.

...And Support Groups?

You may also find it helpful to attend a support group. There are general purpose support groups designed to help people with a variety of psychological problems, and there are anxiety support groups which have a more specific focus - anxiety problems in general, or specific anxiety disorders such as Panic Disorder, Obsessive Compulsive Disorder, etc.

I think most people with a clearly defined anxiety disorder are better served by a support group which focuses specifically on their kind of problem, if such a group is available. However, there are also some good "general purpose" groups, such as Recovery International.

Step Four:

Identify Qualified Therapists

If you decide to get professional help, be prepared to do some work to find a good therapist. You can start by getting the names of therapists in your area who offer the kind of treatment you seek. The websites of the Anxiety Disorders Association of America and the Association for Behavioral and Cognitive Therapies offer a "therapist finder" section to help you find a specialist in your area. The sites for the Obsessive Compulsive Foundation and the TLC Foundation (compulsive behaviors such as hair pulling, skin picking, and nail biting) offer similar lists of professionals who specialize in those areas.

You will probably be better off if you can find a therapist who has specialized training and experience with the anxiety disorder for which you seek help. However, be aware that these lists will generally include any therapist who wishes to be included; they are not a licensing or accreditation process, simply a place to start. You still need to be an informed consumer.

Step Five:

Select a Therapist and Begin Treatment

An initial evaluation with a therapist may take anywhere from one to two sessions. It should enable the therapist to learn enough about you to give you some feedback about your situation and how that therapist proposes to help you, and should also give you a chance to ask more q uestions. One area you should certainly discuss with the therapist is what to expect in treatment, i.e., how will you know it is working? What would be a sign that it is not working?

You will probably also want to know how long treatment will take. What I tell new patients is that, while I can't immediately predict how long their particular situation will require, I do expect that they will have a gut feeling that we are moving in the right direction within the first month of weekly sessions, and that they should see some progress within the first two months. If this doesn't happen, it's a sign that something isn't working right, and we should figure out what's wrong.

CHAPTER ONE

COGNITIVE BEHAVIORAL THERAPY

The brain is a fascinating, time-saving beast. It has fast-tracked responses to certain situations so you don't even have to think about reacting, you just do. This becomes a problem, though, when your automatic response is one of fear in situations where, in reality, there's nothing to be afraid of.

It could be that you go into a state of panic every time you're called in to a meeting with your boss, because years ago, you lost your job in a similar way. Maybe you constantly overreact to innocuous comments from your other half, because you're scared they're going to leave you the same way your ex did. Or it could be that walking to the bus stop is riddled with anxiety thanks to your neighbour's Great Dane, which you believe will one day escape and attack you.

If you're tired of feeling this way, scientists say you can retrain the part of the brain that's responsible for this reaction. It's called the amygdala, and it's an almond-shaped collection of neurons located in each side lobe of the brain.

"It's a part of the brain that occurs in animals and humans," Dr Fiona Kumfor, research officer at Neuroscience Research Australia, says. "So it's not this high level cognitive process that we associate with being human in terms of reasoning and thinking rationally. The amygdala is a very automatic part of the brain that helps us respond to our environment and it seems to be important for registering emotional information."

The brain is primed to quickly identify emotional stimuli, especially when we're in a dangerous situation, so that we can then act fast. "But in a modern lifestyle we're not really being confronted with tigers that we need to run away from". "Instead, it might be stress from work, or that you're never fully relaxed, and your body can then be in this hyper-aroused state where the amygdala is overworking. You might be interpreting emotional cues in the environment in a more exaggerated sense than needed."

Luckily, the brain is plastic and can be retrained. "Potentially, if we can retrain the amygdala, we can regulate these emotions so they're deployed in appropriate situations and not impacting on everyday life and mental health," Kumfor adds.

Shrinking the amygdala

A regular meditation practice of 30 minutes a day has been shown to reduce the size of the amygdala, allowing your rational thinking brain to take over, according to neuroscientists at Harvard University in the US. But which meditation is best? Associate psychologist David R Vago, from the Functional Neuroimaging Laboratory at Harvard Medical School, is an expert in the neuroscience of mindfulness. There are three practices that are best for a sustainable healthy mind.

The first is 'focused attention', where you concentrate on a single object, like a sound, the breath or how your body feels. The second is 'open monitoring', in which you become aware of your thoughts (see our example, right). The third is 'loving kindness', a traditional Buddhist practice in which you cultivate compassion – even for people you don't really like.

To try one of these approaches, do a search online for a guided meditation. Start small with only five minutes a day and slowly increase your practice time.

Unlearning the fear response

Another way to retrain the amygdala is through exposure therapy. As the amygdala is associated with fear, this approach can help those with anxiety, phobias, chronic pain or post-traumatic stress disorder, Dr Sylvia Gustin, senior neuroscientist at Neuroscience Research Australia, says. "In this technique we develop a fear hierarchy, which you then gradually work through to the most fearful situation," she explains.

The way it works is you list all the things that trigger your anxiety, then rank them in order of least to most unnerving. Rather than avoiding all these situations (which would mean the amygdala isn't retrained so it remains overstimulated) you start by exposing yourself to the smallest trigger. Once you're comfortable with that, you work your way up the list so that you can unlearn the fear response.

Quietening the anxiety

When therapy is combined with mindfulness, it can have even better results. A small-scale US study of war veterans with post-traumatic stress disorder found that those who completed group therapy along with mindfulness training showed a shift in their brain activity. The University of Michigan Medical School researchers found the areas of the brain in the regions that dealt with threats, including the amygdala, weren't as active as they previously were.

Gustin is also an advocate of mindful practices, like yoga, to help decrease the activity of the amygdala, but acknowledges that strong anxiety can make it hard to focus. In those cases she says to be patient and stick with it: "We only heal ourselves when we treat ourselves nicely."

Do this daily

Psychotherapist Dr Timothy Stokes says this 'open monitoring' practice is ideal for retraining the amygdala: "The most powerful therapeutic tools begin with observing our thoughts and feelings. This practice creates an observer who watches and allays the tendency to get hijacked by problematic thoughts and feelings."

1. Imagine a situation that causes you anxiety or usually leads to you losing your cool, making the image as vivid as possible.

2. Pay attention to the emotions this causes. It could be an unsettled stomach, a sad feeling in your chest or a burning feeling in your torso.

3. Say to yourself: "This energy is just a feeling in my body."

4. Repeat steps one to three for up to 30 minutes.

4 things to do when anxiety strikes

Follow these steps from meditation expert and Zen teacher Diane Musho Hamilton…

1. Stay present Notice how your body is responding to the situation or perceived threat you're encountering.

2. Let go of the story Empty the mind of thoughts and judgement. This will break the loop between the mind and body.

3. Focus Is part of your body tight, shaking or painful? Focus on these sensations without trying to control or change them.

4. Breathe Aim for a consistent series of rhythmic, smooth and even breaths. This will allow you to centre yourself.

Still anxious? Try this…

Tapping

Tap your temples, cheeks or shoulders repeatedly until you calm down. The mild brain stimulation from the tapping helps to erase the physical basis for a fear memory in the amygdala, a study published in the journal Traumatology found. It doesn't matter if you tap one side or both. You can also try this the day before a stressful event.

Basking in blue

Picture the amygdala inside your skull. Now imagine it's glowing with soft blue light. Visualise the healing light pouring into your frontal lobes and gently setting off billions of neural pathways. This should help you better control your response to the situation that's causing the panic and foster a sense of calm.

Imagining a feather

Close your eyes and use your mind's eye to imagine a feather gently tickling the surface of your amygdala. This will help minimise the fear or anxiety you're feeling and stimulate a series of positive responses from the brain instead.

Proven Tricks For Overcoming Anxiety And Fear

Back in the earlier days of evolution, humans were prey to giant hyenas, cave bears, and predatory kangaroos.

We've been able to outlast those guys, but evolutionary psychologists will tell you that we're still on constant lookout for the thing that wants to eat us next.

The trouble is, the audience at your next presentation is not, in fact, a bunch of razor-toothed animals. They generally want to see you do well.

Since being plagued by anxiety is a sure way to sabotage your own success, we've put together a collection of research-backed tips for overcoming your fears.

Breathe deeply because it lets your nervous system know that it can chill out.

You've probably heard that breathing is a good call if you're stressed out.

But what's fascinating is the reason why it works so well.

"Deep diaphragmatic breathing is a powerful anxiety-reducing technique because it activates the body's relaxation response," explains Psych Central editor Margarita Tartakovsky. "It helps the body go from the fight-or-flight response of the sympathetic nervous system to the relaxed response of the parasympathetic nervous system."

Slowly expose yourself to the things you're afraid of, so they're no longer unfamiliar to you.

If you're trying to get comfortable with negotiating, speaking in public, or other scary activities, psychologists often recommend exposure therapy.

Rehab Institute of Chicago neuroscientist Katherina Hauner has found that it can dramatically improve the way people relate to their fears.

"It is usually done in a series of hierarchical steps, starting with a relatively low level of engagement with the feared situation, and increasing the level with each step," she told the Huffington Post.

"For exposure therapy with a dog phobia," she says, "we might start with just looking at a very small puppy from many feet away, and eventually work our way up to petting a very large dog."

Recognize when you're succumbing to 'misplaced' anxiety, and let it go.

As Wharton research scholar Jeremy Yip has found, fear about one thing in your life has a way of spilling over into other parts of your life.

If you have car trouble on your way to work, there's a good chance that feeling of anxiety will carry over into your workday.

You might feel less confident about pitching your boss on a new project because when you ask yourself, "How do I feel about this?" your general feelings of anxiety make you more risk-averse.

To deal with that, try and recognize where the fear is coming from. If you're worried because you need to make improvements, listen to that. If you're worried because your exhaust is making funny noises, don't.

Spend time with your friends — social support reduces anxiety.

Three decades of research shows that people with close friends are better able to survive divorces, job losses, and other traumatic events.

"Friendfluence" author Carlin Flora says that friendship has long been an evolutionary advantage.

"When we lived in groups where survival itself was difficult, you needed someone who would be guaranteed to throw you a lifeline," she told Thought Catalog. "You can easily theorize that the notion of a best friend developed because we needed someone where we were number one on their list and they were number one on our list in those life and death situations."

Exercise to protect yourself against the effects of stress, which include anxiety and fear.

Working out helps people feel better.

The Mayo Clinic says that exercise helps release anxiety in three main ways:

• Exercise releases brain chemicals associated with easing depression, like endorphins.

• Exercise enhances your immune system, lessening the chance of depression.

• Exercise increases body temperature, which helps people calm down.

And a pro tip: If you're new to working out, psychologists say that "taking away the choice" of whether you're going exercise is the key to sticking to a workout plan.

Reframe anxiety as excitement so that you can devote more energy and resources to the situation.

Harvard Business School assistant professor Alison Wood Brooks has found that the best way to work with anxiety isn't to keep calm — but to get excited.

Emotions happen at two levels: There's the physical sensation, called arousal in the psych world, and then the way you mentally interpret it, called valence.

When you're anxious, your heart rate goes up — that's high arousal. And you read it as bad news — that's a negative valence.

The takeaway: If you're anxious, reframe it as excitement, since you can stay in that high arousal state but read it as good news instead. In experiments, that tactic makes people better public speakers and karaoke singers.

Prevent yourself from always focusing on the negatives by looking at the big picture.

Here's a simple, age-old exercise from Swiss psychiatrist Paul Dubois. Every night, grab a piece of paper and draw two columns. List the things that troubled you in one, and things that were favorable in the other. Make at least one favorable entry for each troubling one.

The realization that you have good things happening every day helps prevent you from just thinking about the negatives.

A few times every day, recognize that at this very moment you're doing OK.

Neurospsychologist Rick Hanson says in his Psychology Today column that our humaninstincts of survival make us constantly unsettled and fearful, protecting us against ever completely letting our guard down.

But it's all a lie, according to Hanson. Your brain is automatically telling you something bad is going to happen, which may be true in the future, but not right now. By reminding yourself that you're OK right now, you can more easily settle your fear and build well-being.

Realize that not everything is the end of the world; one way to do this is by consciously trivializing tasks.

Social psychologist Susan K. Perry suggests in her Psychology Today column that you always think of yourself as playing. If something goes wrong, you can just try again, or try it in some other way.

And when you compare something in your daily life to decisions that are truly life-and-death, it gives you better perspective as to what's really important — and that failure at something that's probably just trivial isn't something to be so fearful or anxious about.

CHAPTER TWO

EXERCISES DESIGNED TO DEAL WITH ANXIETY

How a person deals with other human beings is a big factor in whether or not he or she succeeds in business and life. It involves emotional intelligence (EI), or the ability to recognize and appropriately react to feelings in yourself and the people around you, particularly when it comes to handling stress and frustration. According to Gustavo Oliveira--a consultant who has helped about 2,000 people worldwide improve their EI using something called The DeRose Method--it's a skill everyone can sharpen. Here are his words on four ways to build your emotional intelligence.

Study yourself.

To get a better understanding of your emotional responses, behaviors, and where your weaknesses may lie, learn to pay attention to your reactions and behaviors. And ask people close to you--only if they'll be honest--to tell you what areas of your personality need work.

Manage emotions during stressful situations by breathing correctly.

Deep and steady breathing through the nose with a relaxed ribcage is one of the best ways to lower stress in the body, and strong medicine for anxiety, fear and anger. Deep breathing sends a message to your brain to calm down and relax. The brain then sends this message to your body, resulting in a lower heart rate and blood pressure. And when you are relaxed and calm you can better manage your immediate emotions.

Channel your emotions.

One powerful method of handling negative emotions is to transform negative energies into positive ones by redirecting them to fuel new opportunities. For example, in 2009 I was expanding two successful businesses. Two years later, both had failed and my money was gone. I was crushed, frustrated and disappointed, but instead of letting my emotions reinforce an unproductive mindset and behaviors, I took a five-hour drive and started thinking about ways I could channel the power of frustration into something positive. During this time, I realized that my failures actually taught me many valuable lessons on how to run a business and the things that must be avoided. I decided to teach these lessons to others and created a course which was a huge success and became an amazing new asset.

Transmute your emotions.

Try to transform negative feelings such as anger, hatred, pain, and jealousy into positive ones such as, love, admiration, compassion and kindness. For example, I had a student who was a professional stand-up paddle (SUP) athlete and would become emotionally unstable every time a competitor provoked him during competitions, which would negatively impact his performance. So, I created a behavioral training response for him: I asked him to smile at the competitor, row harder and intensify his focus. With time and training his response improved drastically and his new and unexpected behavior destabilized the competitors who provoked him.

Envy is another common negative emotion. Some of my students have admitted that the achievements of others make them feel as though if they are not good enough. I train them to transform the feeling and substitute it with admiration for the person's success. They come to see it as an opportunity to learn from the person's strengths, which is a more useful and productive response.

Anxiety Disorders Treatment - Phobias

Most anxiety disorders are readily treatable with a combination of psychotherapy and medication. Learn the details of these treatments and other treatment options for generalized anxiety disorder, panic disorder, agoraphobia, social phobia, specific phobia, and post-traumatic stress disorder/acute stress disorder. Treatments for anxiety depend upon the specific disorder diagnosed by a trained mental health professional. Below you will find some general treatment guidelines for different Anxiety Disorders.

This document deals with the treatment of Phobias (fears). Other available documents deal with the treatment of Panic-Related Anxiety (including Agoraphobia), Trauma and Generalized Anxiety

Social Phobia

Social phobia is the most common anxiety disorder in the population. Both men and women experience it equally. The greatest single fear that exists for people is the fear of giving a public presentation or talk, which is a symptom of social phobia. This is because at the root of social phobia is the excessive fear of either being scrutinized by others or of performing a behavior out of anxiety in front of others that might be embarrassing or humiliating, such as speaking unclearly, trembling, or even blushing.

For those suffering from social phobia it can greatly affect the quality of their lives. Oftentimes, because of the extreme anxiety those with social phobia experience during interactions with others, they avoid many social opportunities. Some have had their career potential significantly thwarted if their career advancement has rested upon giving public presentations or developing career networking relationships. Others with social phobia struggle with feelings of loneliness because their social anxiety gets in the way of pursuing dating opportunities or they may avoid social gatherings such as parties.

Social phobia can often be confused with shyness. However, for the majority of those suffering with social phobia they tend not to be shy around those they are familiar with; they can even be quite outgoing when there is not the fear of making an impression on someone whose opinion of them is unknown. Also, those with social phobia experience an extremely high level of anxiety in social situations that far exceeds the discomfort that shy people experience in social situations.

Up until recently, not much was known or understood about social phobia, especially in terms of how to treat it. We now know that people who suffer from social phobia tend to misinterpret neutral social clues so that they think others are negatively evaluating them. They are also very concerned with making a positive impression on people because they greatly desire approval from others. They often doubt their own abilities to be able to be successful in making a good impression. Fortunately, we now have effective therapy interventions to treat those with social phobia.

Psychotherapy

The treatment of choice for social phobia is cognitive behavioral therapy within a group setting called CBGT (cognitive behavioral group therapy). The ideal treatment group size for CBGT includes six patients and two therapists. This treatment relies on a triad of cognitive behavioral interventions, which include: simulated exposures to feared situations through role-plays, cognitive restructuring, and homework assignments done in in vivo exposure.

Before group treatment begins, the patient meets with the therapist and a rank-ordered hierarchy of the patient's most to least feared social situations is constructed. The group creates simulated scenarios in which the patient is exposed to his/her least feared social situations and as the patient is able to conquer these scenarios, moves up on his/her hierarchy list. If the patient begins to feel anxious or increased physiological arousal during a simulated situation, the patient is taught to use a variety of relaxation techniques, such as deep breathing to reduce the anxiety. It is through these simulated exposures that patients are able to face their fears and work through them in a monitored, safe setting.

The second component of CBGT is cognitive therapy. This is very effective since researchers have discovered that social phobia is largely born out of irrational beliefs that people develop over time. The cognitive beliefs of someone with social phobia are based upon the possibility of being negatively evaluated by others, which leads to strong feelings of vulnerability. Also, because those with social phobia tend to have a strong need for approval from others, they fear that they lack the self-esteem, social skills, or ability to make a good social impression on people.

During the first few sessions of CBGT the therapist educates the patients about cognitive therapy and how they can learn to replace their irrational beliefs that lead to anxiety or fear with healthy beliefs. Throughout the simulated scenarios, the group members can then challenge each other's irrational beliefs. By being able to point out to a group member during a simulated exposure that the member's self-perception about how they are coming across in a social situation is distorted, it offers important cognitive restructuring in the moment. CBGT is a careful balancing act between exposure and periods of cognitive restructuring.

The third component of CBGT is having the patients carry out in vivo homework assignments. This means that once the patient has mastered a feared scenario in the group setting, that the patient then goes and exposes himself/herself to a real-life similarly feared scenario, such as giving a presentation or going to a party. This allows for the skills that the patient learns in the group to be transferred to real-life situations.

There are many advantages that the group setting offers to those suffering from social phobia as compared to receiving individual therapy. First, those with various degrees of social phobia can learn vicariously through each other how to effectively handle their fears in social situations. Second, it helps group participants to realize that there are other people with similar fears and problems. This realization helps to reduce participants' fears that their problems are unique and mysterious. Third, by participating in a group treatment it helps to strengthen the patient's public commitment to change. Fourth, a group offers multiple partners with whom role-plays can be practiced. Fifth, a group offers a range of participants who can provide invaluable feedback to each other to help challenge the participant's irrational beliefs underlying their anxiety.

Since a person with social phobia has usually been struggling with the disorder for many years, 3 months of CBGT is not going to completely rid a person of social phobia; however, a reduction in the patient's symptoms should be evident. If after the twelve weeks of CBGT the patient's social phobia has not improved, then it is recommended that the patient continue either in another CBGT group and/or receive individualized psychotherapy treatment. If the person's anxiety within the feared social situations is severe enough to produce panic attacks, then panic control techniques and education about panic attacks should supplement the person's treatment. (See treatment for panic disorder). If the person really does have weak social skills, then social skills training as a supplemental treatment intervention would be quite helpful. Another treatment alternative to try after engaging in CBGT is psychotropic medication.

Medication

Medication for social phobia should be considered as a second line treatment after effective cognitive behavioral treatment has been attempted. Some medications can be helpful in the treatment of someone with social phobia in which cognitive behavioral therapy has been unsuccessful. The medications that have proven to be most successful in treating social phobia are the antidepressant medications called MAOIs (monoamine oxidase inhibitors), such as phenelzine (Nardil). The MAOIs seem to work best for generalized social fears. However, taking MAOIs requires many dietary restrictions because certain foods containing the pressor amine, Tyramine, such as the majority of cheeses, alcoholic beverages, and yeast products can produce an adverse reaction with the medication causing dangerously high blood pressure.

For more specific forms of social phobia such as public speaking and performance anxiety the beta-blockers, such as atenolol have been successful. These provide the convenience of only having to take them just a few hours before the specific anxiety provoking event. However, these medications have not proven to be very successful for severe generalized social phobia.

Recently, the SSRI anti-depressant medication called Paroxetine (Paxil) has received attention for reducing the symptoms of social phobia. This medication generally has few side effects and can be taken for more severe generalized forms of social phobia.

Specific Phobia

Specific phobias are the most prevalent anxiety disorders within the population. They occur when a person develops an irrational fear to a specified object or situation and feels a great degree of anxiety or even has a panic attack when exposed to that feared object or situation. Approximately five to twelve percent of the population has a specific phobia with slightly more women than men being affected by a phobia. Phobias that develop during childhood are usually outgrown by adolescence. Most specific phobias develop during adolescence or adulthood in a person's mid-twenties.

A phobia can develop in a person at anytime as a reaction to a traumatic incident. For example, if a person is in an accident that occurs on a bridge the experience may create a phobia of bridges. Sometimes people can develop a phobia by witnessing something bad happening to another person. For example, witnessing a person being bitten by a snake might create a phobia of snakes in the person who witnessed the incident. People can also develop phobias from hearing about information that might frighten them, such as a person who hears an in-depth story about a plane crash on the news might then develop a phobia of flying. People who have a specific phobia are aware that their level of fear and anxiety about the feared object or situation is unreasonable.

The most common subtypes of specific phobias are: animal, including animals and insects; natural environment, including bad weather, water, and heights; blood-injection-injury, including seeing blood from an injury, injection, or medical procedure; situational, including bridges, flying, using public transportation, and tunnels.

The most common situation that people fear most is actually public speaking. However a fear of public speaking is categorized under social phobia. This is because the primary feature of social phobia is a fear of being in a situation in which a person will be evaluated by others or somehow do something that will cause humiliation and/or embarrassment to oneself in public. Public speaking is more about the fear of being under public scrutiny, than fearing a specific situation based solely on irrational fears of that situation.

Specific phobias usually tend not to cause much disruption in a person's life. Most people are able to lead normal lives easily able to avoid whatever specific situation or object the person fears. For example, if a person has a phobia of snakes it is unlikely that being afraid of snakes will disrupt the person's life, unless the person is a forest ranger or works in the snake collection at a zoo. However, a specific phobia can become a problem for people who have to travel by plane regularly for business and have a fear of flying, or are afraid of elevators and have to use an elevator on a daily basis either for professional or personal reasons.

Fortunately, specific phobias are very treatable. The treatment of choice consists of cognitive behavioral interventions. Medication may be used in an adjunctive manner depending upon the severity of the phobia.

Psychotherapy As A Treatment

Psychotherapy is the treatment of choice for specific phobias. Cognitive behavioral treatment interventions including exposure, systematic desensitization, cognitive re-structuring, and relaxation techniques include the best approach to treat specific phobia.

Exposure therapy is the most effective therapy treatment technique for specific phobia. This intervention entails exposing the patient to the feared situations or objects for continuous periods of time. This way the patient is forced to confront his/her fears within the context of therapeutic management. The patient starts with situations that are the least anxiety provoking, such as seeing pictures of snakes, and works up through a hierarchy of gradually more difficult scenarios to most anxiety producing, such as holding a snake. The patient is taught a variety of relaxation techniques such as progressive muscle relaxation and deep breathing so that the patient can control anxiety levels during exposure to the feared object or situation.

Systematic desensitization is another widely used intervention for specific phobia. It involves having the patient imagine being exposed to the feared object or situation. Again, the patient begins with the least anxiety producing scenarios and works up to the most anxiety producing scenarios. The patient is encouraged to imagine very specific details associated with the feared object or situation such as smells, tastes, sounds, visual cues, and touch in order to make it as real as possible. Relaxation techniques are used to moderate anxiety levels. Studies have indicated that exposure to the feared scenarios in a person's imagination is an effective technique for conquering specific phobias.

Cognitive therapy is also helpful to people with specific phobia since their fears about a particular object or situation are based on irrational beliefs.

Using cognitive therapy, the therapist helps the patient to identify what the irrational beliefs are that the person holds to be true about the feared object or situation. Then the therapist helps the patient replace the irrational beliefs with more realistic or adaptive beliefs about the feared object or place. Sometimes this may also require educating the patient with correct information about whatever it is the patient fears. For example, a person's phobia of flying may be fueled by not understanding how an airplane works and the extensive training that airline pilots have. By educating the patient with this information it can help the patient form more realistic beliefs that help reduce the patient's fear.

Medications As A Treatment

There are not currently any psychotropic medications used just to treat specific phobia. Medications should only be used as an adjunctive treatment approach if the person is experiencing moderate to severe anxiety or panic when in the presence of the feared object or situation. Another factor to consider is how often the person is confronted with the feared object or situation. For instance, if the person is phobic of elevators and must use an elevator every day for work then medication is more strongly indicated. Also, the use of medication will depend on whether or not the person is effectively able to reduce their anxiety with relaxation techniques.

If medication is indicated for a specific phobia than the anti-anxiety benzodiazepine agents such as Alprazolam (Xanax) or Clonazepam (Klonopin) would be the drug of choice. This is because they are short acting, which means they work quickly to relieve anxiety, so they do not have to build up in a person's body over time to be effective. Also, since they are short acting they leave a person's system quickly so that the person does not have to deal with ongoing negative side effects of being on a continuous medication.

It is important to use benzodiazepines carefully, however, because they are highly physically and psychologically addictive. They should not be prescribed to anyone who has any prior history of addictions and/or substance abuse. These medications need to be prescribed and used with caution.

CHAPTER THREE

FEAR IN THE BRAIN

Fear may be as old as life on Earth. It is a fundamental, deeply wired reaction, evolved over the history of biology, to protect organisms against perceived threat to their integrity or existence. Fear may be as simple as a cringe of an antenna in a snail that is touched, or as complex as existential anxiety in a human.

Whether we love or hate to experience fear, it's hard to deny that we certainly revere it – devoting an entire holiday to the celebration of fear.

Thinking about the circuitry of the brain and human psychology, some of the main chemicals that contribute to the "fight or flight" response are also involved in other positive emotional states, such as happiness and excitement. So, it makes sense that the high arousal state we experience during a scare may also be experienced in a more positive light. But what makes the difference between getting a "rush" and feeling completely terrorized?

We are psychiatrists who treat fear and study its neurobiology. Our studies and clinical interactions, as well as those of others, suggest that a major factor in how we experience fear has to do with the context. When our "thinking" brain gives feedback to our "emotional" brain and we perceive ourselves as being in a safe space, we can then quickly shift the way we experience that high arousal state, going from one of fear to one of enjoyment or excitement.

When you enter a haunted house during Halloween season, for example, anticipating a ghoul jumping out at you and knowing it isn't really a threat, you are able to quickly relabel the experience. In contrast, if you were walking in a dark alley at night and a stranger began chasing you, both your emotional and thinking areas of the brain would be in agreement that the situation is dangerous, and it's time to flee!

But how does your brain do this?

Fear reaction starts in the brain and spreads through the body to make adjustments for the best defense, or flight reaction. The fear response starts in a region of the brain called the amygdala. This almond-shaped set of nuclei in the temporal lobe of the brain is dedicated to detecting the emotional salience of the stimuli – how much something stands out to us.

For example, the amygdala activates whenever we see a human face with an emotion. This reaction is more pronounced with anger and fear. A threat stimulus, such as the sight of a predator, triggers a fear response in the amygdala, which activates areas involved in preparation for motor functions involved in fight or flight. It also triggers release of stress hormones and sympathetic nervous system.

This leads to bodily changes that prepare us to be more efficient in a danger: The brain becomes hyperalert, pupils dilate, the bronchi dilate and breathing accelerates. Heart rate and blood pressure rise. Blood flow and stream of glucose to the skeletal muscles increase. Organs not vital in survival such as the gastrointestinal system slow down.

A part of the brain called the hippocampus is closely connected with the amygdala. The hippocampus and prefrontal cortex help the brain interpret the perceived threat. They are involved in a higher-level processing of context, which helps a person know whether a perceived threat is real.

For instance, seeing a lion in the wild can trigger a strong fear reaction, but the response to a view of the same lion at a zoo is more of curiosity and thinking that the lion is cute. This is because the hippocampus and the frontal cortex process contextual information, and inhibitory pathways dampen the amygdala fear response and its downstream results. Basically, our "thinking" circuitry of brain reassures our "emotional" areas that we are, in fact, OK.

Similar to other animals, we very often learn fear through personal experiences, such as being attacked by an aggressive dog, or observing other humans being attacked by an aggressive dog.

However, an evolutionarily unique and fascinating way of learning in humans is through instruction – we learn from the spoken words or written notes! If a sign says the dog is dangerous, proximity to the dog will trigger a fear response.

We learn safety in a similar fashion: experiencing a domesticated dog, observing other people safely interact with that dog or reading a sign that the dog is friendly.

Fear creates distraction, which can be a positive experience. When something scary happens, in that moment, we are on high alert and not preoccupied with other things that might be on our mind (getting in trouble at work, worrying about a big test the next day), which brings us to the here and now.

Furthermore, when we experience these frightening things with the people in our lives, we often find that emotions can be contagious in a positive way. We are social creatures, able to learn from one another. So, when you look over to your friend at the haunted house and she's quickly gone from screaming to laughing, socially you're able to pick up on her emotional state, which can positively influence your own.

While each of these factors - context, distraction, social learning - have potential to influence the way we experience fear, a common theme that connects all of them is our sense of control. When we are able to recognize what is and isn't a real threat, relabel an experience and enjoy the thrill of that moment, we are ultimately at a place where we feel in control. That perception of control is vital to how we experience and respond to fear. When we overcome the initial "fight or flight" rush, we are often left feeling satisfied, reassured of our safety and more confident in our ability to confront the things that initially scared us.

It is important to keep in mind that everyone is different, with a unique sense of what we find scary or enjoyable. This raises yet another question: While many can enjoy a good fright, why might others downright hate it?

Any imbalance between excitement caused by fear in the animal brain and the sense of control in the contextual human brain may cause too much, or not enough, excitement. If the individual perceives the experience as "too real," an extreme fear response can overcome the sense of control over the situation.

This may happen even in those who do love scary experiences: They may enjoy Freddy Krueger movies but be too terrified by "The Exorcist," as it feels too real, and fear response is not modulated by the cortical brain.

On the other hand, if the experience is not triggering enough to the emotional brain, or if is too unreal to the thinking cognitive brain, the experience can end up feeling boring. A biologist who cannot tune down her cognitive brain from analyzing all the bodily things that are realistically impossible in a zombie movie may not be able to enjoy "The Walking Dead" as much as another person.

So if the emotional brain is too terrified and the cognitive brain helpless, or if the emotional brain is bored and the cognitive brain is too suppressing, scary movies and experiences may not be as fun.

All fun aside, abnormal levels of fear and anxiety can lead to significant distress and dysfunction and limit a person's ability for success and joy of life.

Nearly one in four people experiences a form of anxiety disorder during their lives, and nearly 8 percent experience post-traumatic stress disorder (PTSD).

Disorders of anxiety and fear include phobias, social phobia, generalized anxiety disorder, separation anxiety, PTSD and obsessive compulsive disorder. These conditions usually begin at a young age, and without appropriate treatment can become chronic and debilitating and affect a person's life trajectory. The good news is that we have effective treatments that work in a relatively short time period, in the form of psychotherapy and medications.

CHAPTER FOUR

SUREFIRE WAYS TO GET RID OF BAD HABITS

Success, happiness and good health often elude us not because we lack good habits but because we have bad habits. Sometimes they are habits like procrastination or mindless spending. But at other times they can be addictions like smoking and gambling.

Knowing how our bad habits negatively influence our lives is rarely enough to break them. For example, all smokers are aware of the health consequences of smoking. Diseased lungs are displayed prominently in every cigarette pack. There would be no smokers in the world today if that worked.

This fails to work because we don't do our bad habits for the reasons we should not do them. No smoker has ever smoked a cigarette to get cancer. Students don't procrastinate to fail. So in order to break our bad habits, we must first remove the reason why we do them. In other words, we need to eliminate the desire to do the habit.

Once the desire is gone, it takes no willpower to break bad habits, just as it doesn't take willpower to not do things we have no desire to do. It doesn't take much effort to stop yourself from eating live frogs because you have no desire to do it. Breaking your bad habits can be just as effortless. You just need the right belief and the right system.

Our Habits Controls Us

From the outside, it would seem that our bad habits is a matter of choice. Smokers, for example, do make the choice of trying their first cigarette. But no smoker has ever made a decision that they will keep smoking for the rest of their lives. We often fall into the trap thinking we can stop whenever we want, only to realize that we no longer have any control. When we watch the first episode of a TV show, we end up binge watching multiple seasons at a stretch because we cannot stop ourselves. Every addict wishes inside that he had never started because life was fine before their addiction but now they are hooked and cannot enjoy life without satisfying their craving.

Researchers from National Institute on Alcohol Abuse and Alcoholism trained rats to press a lever to get a piece food. The researchers later electrified the floor so that when the rat walked to get the food, it received a shock. In a different experimental setting, the rat recognized the danger in the electric floor and would avoid it. But when the rat saw the lever, the habits took over and the rat would press the lever and go for the food and get electrocuted every time. The rat could not stop itself in spite of being aware of the danger because the habits were so strong.

Similarly, dieters find it hard to resist junk, smokers struggle to quit and students procrastinate on their assignments in spite of being aware of the consequences it has on their lives. Strong habits create an obsessive craving which makes our brain behave on autopilot even if there are strong disincentives like loss of job, health, reputation, family or home.

When We Use Willpower to Quit, We Fail

We usually try to break bad habits using willpower, which makes us feel we are making a sacrifice. A Harvard study showed the 12 month success rates of people who used the willpower method to quit smoking with no education or support was 6%.

When using willpower to quit, we find life extremely unpleasant and difficult and have to be cautious all the time to prevent relapse. This is because the desire to do the habit always remains inside us.

10 % of former smokers who abstained from smoking for ten years showed ongoing cravings even years later. 3 Mere abstinence does not mean we have broken our habit. It just means we don't allow ourselves to do our habit. A person who does not drink alcohol but who is constantly thinking about alcohol is not a non-alcoholic but is an alcoholic who does not let himself drink.

We see the benefits of breaking our habits but also believe it provides us with something which we are now depriving ourselves of. This makes us miserable, vulnerable and increases desire that begins to obsess us. We try to overcome this by not thinking about our craving but that only makes us more obsessed.

Believing our problems can be easily solved by doing our bad habits we begin to question our decision to break our bad habits. Finally, we accept defeat and cave in. This minor relapse makes us feel bad and we indulge in the very same habit that made us feel bad, to feel better.

We fail to break our bad habits not because we lack willpower but because we don't eliminate desire. Without desire, willpower is not required to stop, just as it doesn't take willpower to not do the things we have no desire to do.

Why Does Our Brain Form Habits If They Are Bad?

Habits is a way for the brain to save effort by making rewarding behaviour automatic. Without habits, you will have to relearn how to brush your teeth every morning. Habits are useful but the problem is our brain cannot tell the difference between good and bad habits. Behavior that gives us short-term rewards often becomes habits, even if they cause long-term harm. Overeating, procrastinating and smoking becomes habit easily because the rewards are instant and the pain comes later. Developing the habit of exercising is harder because the reward comes later.

Schultz from the University of Cambridge, trained a monkey named Julio to pull a lever when a shape appeared on computer screen. Pulling the lever gave Julio a drop of blackberry juice which made the pleasure centres of his brain light up. When his brain started craving for the juice, Julio was glued to the monitor like a gambler in a slot machine. If the juice arrived late or diluted, this craving would turn into anger & depression.

Charles Duhigg's book, "The Power of Habit" focuses on the 3 components of a habit. The first component is the trigger, which tells the brain to start doing a particular behaviour (shapes in Julio's monitor). The second component is the behaviour that is done (Julio pulling the lever). The third part is the reward for doing the behaviour (Julio's blackberry juice). The habit is formed when the brain starts to crave for the reward as soon as the brain sees the trigger. There is nothing programmed in our brains that makes us want to overeat or smoke. But over time we slowly develop a neurological craving for these things.

Break The Habit By Seeing The Reward As An Illusion

The first step to breaking your bad habit is identifying the reward.

What do you really get doing your habit?

If the rewards you think your habits provided were actually real, then you can break your bad habits, simply by switching your existing habit with a healthier behavior that provided the same reward. For example, if you eat junk at work for distraction, then you can break your habit simply by replacing eating junk with a healthier distraction that does not add to your waistline. This is the premise of the book "The Power of Habit" and this works well for weaker habits. But try telling a smoker to resist his urge for smoking when he is bored by entertaining himself on YouTube. He won't be a successful non-smoker for very long. This is because most rewards of our habits are illusions.

We often rationalize why we do our bad habits but all the reasons we use to justify our behaviour are an illusion, excuses, fallacies or based on myth. For example, smokers believe they need cigarettes to relax, relieve stress, to concentrate or to relieve boredom. But cigarettes do not give them any of this. If it did, they should be a lot more relaxed, focused and less bored than non-smokers.

Most of us brainwash ourselves in a certain way that keeps us doing our bad habits. Only by identifying what we think is the reward can we address and remove the myths we have about the reward. When we begin to see through the illusory rewards, we eliminate desire by realizing that there is nothing to give up.

What We Give Up When We Break Bad Habits?

What are we giving up when we break our bad habits? Well, most of the time you are giving up absolutely nothing.

We don't do our bad habits for pleasure. We do it to feel normal. This feels like pleasure. A drug addict feels miserable, anxious, stressed and angry when he is deprived of his drug. When he shoots up his drug, he gets relief from all the negative symptoms. The subsequent dose partially relieves the symptoms but also ensures that the addict goes through withdrawal again. This keeps the addict stuck in the vicious habit loop. Normal people do not experience the symptoms of the drug addict. When we look at this it is obvious to us that the symptoms the drug addict experiences are caused by the drug, not removed by it. But we fail to have the same understanding when it comes to our bad habits.

Our bad habits cause symptoms of craving that normal people don't experience. We do our bad habits to partially relieve the symptoms but it only keeps us stuck in the vicious habit loop ensuring we experience the symptoms of craving again.

Unlike drug addiction which might require a visit to rehab, the craving caused by most bad habits including alcohol and smoking can be killed immediately when the belief system is changed. If you are not entirely convinced that there is nothing to give up, you need to examine the rewards of your bad habits and see them for what they really are. Otherwise, you will feel craving and will have to use willpower to prevent relapse.

The 4 Illusory Rewards

If you think your habit provides any of the following 4 rewards, you probably have an illusory reward:

1. Relieves stress

2. Relieves boredom

3. Improves concentration

4. Relieves anxiety and gives confidence

We will address the common myths people have about each of these rewards which will help dispel the illusion.

Reward 1 - Relief From Stress & Relaxation

For many, habits provide relaxation and relief from stress. We all have several things stressing us out. Not just big tragedies but relatively minor things like work deadlines. We do our bad habits to relieve this stress and the stress does seem to go away. But what has really happened?

Apart from the environmental stress, we experience additional stress because of the aggravation caused by craving. Bad habits relieve this portion of stress it created through craving. But our real-world stress like work deadlines continues to exist. When we do our habits we feel better able to cope with this stress because we temporarily don't have the additional stress caused by the craving to deal with.

A study has shown that we fall back into our habits when we are stressed because we feel less anxiety and more in control when we do our habits. People who have been sober for years relapse when a major life catastrophe happens like a death of a loved one or divorce. This is because of a failure to understand that alcohol does not relieve stress but only adds to the problem.

The habits that we fall back on during times of stress need not be bad. In a study, students who habitually ate a healthy breakfast continued to eat healthy during the stressful period of their exams. Whereas students who gained extra weight during their exams had a habit of eating unhealthy. Consciously engineering your habits is important so that your habits make you better and not worse during times of stress.

Reward 2 - Relief From Boredom

Some people do their habit because they are bored. Boredom is a frame of mind and not a physical condition that can be cured. Initially, we are bored. Now we are bored and engaged in self-destructive behaviour. Our bad habits do not cure boredom. It just creates a temporary distraction that allows us to forget that we are bored.

If our bad habits did relieve boredom, then why do we have to engage in it multiple times or do it for longer periods at a stretch?

Most bad habits rob us of our energy and make us more lethargic, putting us in a state of mind where we cannot do anything else. Instead of doing something when bored like how a normal person would, we lounge around, do our bad habit and feel more bored.

If you know someone who plays excessive video games or who spends hours in front of the TV, you will see they are not any less bored. They will be extremely tired and will feel like shit for wasting so much time.

Reward 3 - Helps Concentration & Removes Mental Block

If you think your bad habits removes mental blocks and improves concentration, then you are not alone. Some of the greatest artists of the world including Van Gogh and Beethoven were addicts. But curing addiction does not lower creativity because your genes do not change. It is just your craving that goes away. So what really happens?

A study done on 96 undergraduates showed a reduction in the student's ability to do tasks that required visuospatial memory, when they experienced craving for chocolate. In other words, craving negatively affected the student's ability to remember.

Our bad habits cause craving which creates a distraction that makes it difficult to concentrate. When we need to concentrate we do our habits to eliminate the distraction caused by our craving. We give credit to our bad habits for helping us concentrate when it was responsible for the distraction to begin with. People without bad habits will not have problems with concentration because they don't experience the craving.

Over time people who believe that their bad habits help them concentrate begin to believe that it removes mental blocks. After you do your bad habits, your block will still exist, but only now you will get the job done just like how anybody would have done it. But your bad habits get the credit for helping you get the work done.

Your bad habits provide no mental performance advantage and believing it does is based on fallacy and myth.

Reward 4 - Confidence & Anxiety Relief

We acknowledge the relief provided by our bad habit as it removes the small amount of emptiness and insecurity. But we don't acknowledge that this emptiness and insecurity are the symptoms of our bad habits in the first placek.

People who have had their bad habits for many decades have been in a perpetual state of anxiety and emptiness so their bad habits seem to be the only way to get confidence and a relief from this feeling. Our bad habits do not relieve the anxiety in our lives, it causes it. People without bad habits never feel this insecurity or anxiety, to begin with.

Freedom from the self-loathing and dependency is one of the biggest positive changes people see in their lives when they break their habits. They are more relaxed and confident after breaking their bad habits and are better able to deal with their anxieties if it is not gone altogether.

Relief From Craving is The Only Reward

Craving and withdrawal can make you insecure, irritable, anxious or agitated. Though there is no physical pain, it causes mental agony giving us a feeling that something is not right. For example, smokers believe that withdrawal is a physical trauma caused by not satisfying their craving. But eight hours after putting out the last cigarette, a smoker is 97% nicotine-free. This happens every night during sleep. Only during the day does he feel the need to smoke every hour to fix his craving.

After three days of not smoking, a smoker is 100% nicotine-free. Yet smokers relapse because of craving after months of abstinence. The truth is withdrawal and craving is almost always psychological even for smokers & alcoholics.

We associate our bad habits with pleasure because we see them satisfy our craving, but don't see them causing it. Our craving is not cured by our bad habits but is caused by it.

We might have started doing our bad habits for many reasons, but the only reason why we keeping doing them is to feed the craving. Every time we do our habit, the craving is satisfied temporarily. This provides a temporary relief, putting us in a normal state of mind. But by doing our habit, we have set ourselves up to experience craving again in the future. The more we feed our craving, the more it takes to satisfy it. Smokers go from one cigarette to chain smoking fairly quickly.

What we really enjoy is not our bad habits but the feeling we get when our craving is satisfied. It is like putting on tight shoes just for the pleasure of taking them off. This is why by breaking bad habits, you are giving up nothing.

Hidden Drivers of Bad Habits

Alcoholics Anonymous (AA) have a concept called dry drunk, where alcoholics stop drinking but still remain angry, selfish and narcissistic. Our bad habits are often symptoms of some inner conflict. Things like anger, shame, loneliness, fear and hopelessness that makes people start doing their bad habits, needs to be addressed first. Until the flawed beliefs are fixed, we will always remain vulnerable to relapse. The habit of procrastination, for example, can be fixed only temporarily, if the underlying fear of failure is left unaddressed.

Bad habits are a way for our sub-conscious mind to avoid the real inner conflict that exists inside us. The inner conflict is either a bitter truth ("I am ashamed of my past") or a distorted assumption ("I screw up everything" or "I am better than everybody"). This inner conflict is never a mystery but we make it a mystery because acknowledging the truth is uncomfortable. It is easier to think we have no choice or control over our lives than it is to take responsibility for fixing it.

The best way to fix inner conflicts is through therapy which works by bringing our inner conflict to light causing them to vaporize like a vampire. The next best way is service. Helping others has helped AA members reduce their desire to drink. A study of 195 addicted adolescents showed that treatment showed substantial improvement when it was accompanied by service. 10 This works because love neutralizes shame and service to others reduce obsession and craving by eliminating the inner conflict. Helpfulness may not help break bad habits by itself, but it addresses the internal conflicts that create craving.

The System To Break Bad Habits

Now that we have addressed the core beliefs and issues that make us do our bad habits, let us look at the step by step system to break bad habits. With this system, you will be able to break any habit easily and effortlessly without using willpower.

Helping Others Break Bad Habits

Do not patronize the person you are trying to help, by telling them why their habits are bad. They already know this and don't do their bad habits for the reasons they shouldn't do it. They do their bad habits to feel normal.

Do not tell them breaking bad habits is easy as it will only irritate them. Give them the support and praise to keep them moving forward.

Do not force them to break their bad habits. Even if they try, they will use willpower to quit and end up failing. Tell them that people who succeeded in breaking their habits did not use willpower but instead addressed their flawed beliefs. Tell them how their bad habits only remove their need to do the habit which is perceived as pleasure by the brain. But in reality, their bad habit do not give them anything.

When they start believing that they can break their bad habits, their mind will begin to open up and that is when they are ready to read this book. Mention that there is no pressure to break their bad habits. If they want to continue to do their bad habits after reading this book, they can.

Where To Go From Here

The key to making it easy to break bad habits is to make your decision final and certain. Don't worry whether or not you have broken your bad habit. Know that you have. Do not ever doubt your decision. Celebrate it. Withdrawal is entirely psychological and if you are sulking, it only means you have not addressed your belief systems yet. Revisit Steps 2 to 4 in the system.

Don't make the mistake of procrastinating and not applying what you have learnt. You can wait for as long as you want to break your bad habits but the right time will never come and your habits are not going to be any easier to break tomorrow.

Some people think their bad habits has not caused any problem yet, so it is not a big deal if they don't break their habits now. The best time to fix the roof is when it is not raining. Don't wait for things to go wrong before you fix your bad habits. Break your bad habits now.

CHAPTER FIVE

STRONGER FOR THE EXPERIENCE

Many of us don't realize how much our past is dictating our current and future lives. We think that we're being cautious and smart, that we're using hard-earned information from what happened long ago to avoid the same mistakes now.

Little do we realize that holding onto past occurrences just makes them happen again and again. In this book, I'm going to talk about why we hold onto the past, how it messes with our lives now, and how to let it all go.

The ego is the part of your mind that stays focused on the past. It has a really potent message about the past that it feeds you all the time, and that message is: Watch out, it's going to happen again.

This is one of the sly tricks of the ego; this belief alone is enough to keep you stuck. And it works like a charm.

The fear that what happened in the past is going to happen again makes us so scared that it keeps us from enjoying what is actually happening now. Instead of being open to different experiences and outcomes, we are riddled with fear that we are going to get hurt again.

When our minds are focused on something then it becomes our experience; our expectations become our realities. The reason this is true is because we cannot separate ourselves from our perception. What we perceive is what is real to us. If your perception is stuck on repeat in the past, then your present is repeating in the past too.

It isn't until we actually let go of the past completely that we can really move on and have a new experience. And the way to do that is by surrendering your fears.

You have to become willing to create a different reality. Your life will not turn out differently unless you do something different. And luckily, you can.

Here's how to let go of past fears that are cursing you in the present:

1. Notice when your fear surfaces—the one that says, It's going to happen again.

If we are going to let go of fears we have to recognize them first. Just noticing goes a long way; it's called gaining consciousness.

When you start to feel yourself getting a little anxious or fearful, stop and take notice. Think to yourself, "Oh here it is, I'm starting to get freaked out."

This step helps you start to disengage from the fear as the ultimate reality. It helps you to realize that you are not your fear.

2. Call out the fear.

Get clear about what you are afraid of. What happened? What are you afraid of happening again?

Maybe the fear is that when you opened-up to another person, you felt rejected. Maybe the fear is when you got close to another person, you lost yourself.

Name it (I would even suggest writing it down). Again, knowing what the fear is is the only way you can let it go.

When fear flies under the radar, it has the power to plague us without us even knowing it. If we are constantly inundated with unconscious fears then we start to develop other symptoms--illnesses, physical symptoms, depression, anxiety and other ailments.

If something feels "off," don't be afraid to investigate what's going on. You gain freedom by looking your fears in the eye.

3. Become willing to let the past go through forgiveness.

It always comes back to forgiveness because forgiveness equals letting go.

The things we are holding onto from the past are the things that we have not fully forgiven. They come in the form of resentments, but also just flat-out fears.

The essence of forgiveness is: I know that what happened was a mistake. I know that it happened because we (I, the other person, or both of us) were acting out of fear. I am willing to feel peace about it and let it go.

Big words. So important.

Forgiveness is a life-changing practice. It is absolutely crucial in creating a new reality in your present and future. For a detailed guide on the how to forgive, check out Why Forgiveness Will Change Your Life.

4. Recognize that peace lives in you.

Really. It does.

Often we want the people around us to mold and change so we can feel better. But actually if we are scared of the past (OUR past) then it's our job to regain a sense of peace.

Ideally the people in our lives will support us when we're scared, but ultimately it's not their job to make everything better. Once we realize this, then we stop relying so heavily on others to feel safe.

Prayer and meditation are great tools to bring you back into the present. If you simply close your eyes, feel your breath, and listen to your heart, you can easily re-center and orient yourself back to now.

Fear is only activated when we are focused on the past or the future. Anytime you feel fear, if you can make your way back to now you will realize that you are actually safe and well.

The next time you feel fear coming on, implement all four of these steps. They will help you come back to who you really are, which is a peaceful, joyful, magnificent person.

Just remember, you are much more powerful than your fears; you don't have to keep living them over and over again. When you choose to have a different experience in life, that different experience will also choose you.

CHAPTER SIX

PRACTICING MINDFULNESS MEDIATION

To effectively manage stress and anxiety, you need to calm down your amygdala's fear and panic. A mindfulness mind-set and stress reduction techniques are the antidote to being swept away or immobilized by stress and anxiety. Practicing mindfulness for stress and anxiety is an open, compassionate attitude toward your inner experience that creates a healthy distance between you and your stressful thoughts and anxious feelings, giving you the space to choose how to respond to them.

With mindfulness practice for stress and anxiety, you learn how to sit peacefully with your thoughts and feelings in the present moment, creating an inner calm to help contain and reduce stress and anxiety.

If I had to pick just one tool for dealing with stress and anxiety, I'd choose mindfulness. The use of mindfulness is supported by a growing neuroscientific literature, demonstrating actual changes to neurons in the amygdala following mindfulness training. Mindfulness-based interventions have gained the attention of therapists, educators, coaches, and even politicians and business leaders. This brain skill can have far-reaching beneficial effects, not only transforming brain neurons but improving immunity, health, life, and relationship satisfaction. Mindfulness for anxiety and stress has the potential to make not only individuals but even businesses, institutions, and societies more stress-proof.

In this book, you'll learn about mindfulness, its history in ancient Buddhist philosophy, and the current use in the West of mindfulness exercises as a widely accepted and effective mind-body practice for anxiety and stress reduction. You'll learn the qualities of a mindful mind-set and how to train your mind to be more mindfulthrough mindfulness meditation practice and mind-set change. Read on, and learn why "The Mindful Revolution," as Time magazine dubbed it, is the key to managing your stress and anxiety!

The Roots of Mindfulness

Mindfulness is both a skill and an attitude toward living that originated thousands of years ago as part of Buddhist philosophy. According to the Buddha, mental suffering (or inner stress) occurs because we cling to positive experiences, not wanting them to end, and we strive to avoid pain, sadness, and other negative experiences. This effort to control our mental and bodily experiences is misguided and out of touch with the reality of living. We can never escape loss and suffering because these are natural parts of life. Our experiences are always changing. Living things wither and die, to be replaced by new living things. The forces of nature are beyond human control.

The Buddha believed that although pain is inevitable, suffering is not. Suffering results from our attempts to cling to pleasure and push away pain. Buddhist teaching describes suffering in terms of being shot by two arrows. The first arrow is the pain and stress that are an inevitable part of being human. These types of stressors, such as aging, illness, and death, are beyond our control. The second arrow is the one we use to shoot ourselves in the foot by reacting to the natural experience of human suffering (or stress) with aversion and protest. It's as if we've become phobic of our own emotions! When we begin to feel stressed, we create mental stories of worry and regret that compound our mental suffering. We get caught up in negative beliefs about ourselves, regrets about the past, or worries about the future, taking us out of the present moment. Or we try to push our feelings of stress and anxiety away through addictions and avoidance. These strategies just make things worse. As one of my wisest supervisors once said, "The cover-up is worse than the crime!" Practicing mindfulness for stress and anxiety returns us to the present moment.

The Buddha also believed that if we can understand the nature of suffering and learn to accept pain and loss with compassion (rather than running away from them), our mental suffering will lessen. We may not be able to get rid of the first arrow of inevitable pain and grief, but we can get rid of the second arrow of self-created mental and emotional suffering with mindfulness-based stress-reduction techniques. By looking at our own inner experiences with a curious, nonjudgmental, and welcoming attitude, we can learn to better tolerate negative states of mind (such as feeling stressed and anxious) and relate to these experiences in a more kind, accepting way. Using mindfulness for anxiety and stress, by calibrating us for momentary neutrality, creates space for such tolerance. Another truth about suffering that the Buddha understood is that our thoughts, feelings, and physical sensations, like all other aspects of life, are transient and constantly changing. When we directly face and accept negative experiences, they'll move through us, rather than getting stuck. The Buddha also believed that living a life of peace, self-discipline, service, and compassion would create an end to suffering on a higher level.

University of Massachusetts Medical School professor emeritus Jon Kabat-Zinn was the visionary who first introduced mindfulness practice for stress and anxiety to the Western medical establishment. He reframed the Buddhist concepts using scientific terminology, added some meditation exercises and yoga stretches, and developed an intensive eight-to-ten-week mindfulness-based stress reduction (MBSR) program that included forty minutes of mindfulness meditation practice each day as homework. He recruited into the program a group of chronic-pain patients who weren't responding to regular medical treatment. Incredibly, these participants reported less pain, improved mood, and better mental health from the beginning to end of the mindfulness-based program (Kabat-Zinn 1982; Kabat-Zinn, Lipworth, and Burney 1985), and in comparison to a group of patients receiving the clinic's normal care (Kabat-Zinn, Lipworth, and Burney 1985). And thus the Mindful Revolution was born.

Today, mindfulness-based interventions for pain, stress, depression, anxiety, cancer, addiction, and chronic illness are accepted worldwide. The credibility of mindfulness exercises as an intervention for anxiety and stress and stress-related illness has been enhanced by its strong neuroscientific base. University of Wisconsin professor of psychology and psychiatry Richie Davidson has been instrumental in demonstrating how mindfulness works in the brain and how mindfulness for stress can change brain structure and functioning to facilitate stress resilience and mental health.

Dr. Davidson's research team used brain imaging technology to study mindfulness meditation techniques in Buddhist monks and novice meditators (Davidson et al. 2003; Lutz et al. 2004). Their findings suggest that "contemplative practices" such as meditation and mindfulness can improve compassion, empathy, kindness, and attention in the brain. These studies powerfully demonstrate neuroplasticity—that even adult brains can change their structure and pathways with repeated practice of new habits. By practicing mindfulness techniques for stress, you can learn to redirect the emotional reactivity of your stress response into more calm, peaceful, and attentive states.

Mindfulness and Your Amygdala

Your feelings of stress and anxiety result from your amygdala's seeing external experiences or even your own emotions as threats. This is a problem, both because it's impossible to escape many stressful experiences and because it's impossible to stop stress-related emotions from arising.

The location of your amygdala—in the middle of your brain, beneath your cortex—means that it receives information about threats and initiates your stress response very rapidly, sometimes even before the thinking parts of your brain know what's happening. In other words, you can't stop your amygdala from trying to protect you by initiating a stress response when it senses a change in circumstances that could lead to danger, loss, or pain. And you probably wouldn't want it to! Without your amygdala, you might waltz into traffic, stick your hand on a hot stove, or hang out with unsavory characters without realizing the danger. But you do need to manage your amygdala so that it doesn't compound your stress and anxiety or create unnecessary suffering for you. Using mindfulness techniques for stress and anxiety allows your prefrontal cortex to calm your amygdala when it overreacts, so you can avoid the Buddha's second arrow (unnecessary suffering), resulting in stress reduction.

Mindfulness skills are the antidote to the amygdala's rapid reactivity. With mindfulness techniques for anxiety and stress, you can learn to slow things down long enough for the prefrontal cortex to get on board and steer you through the stressful rough waters. Mindfulness meditation practice also creates a calm, relaxed state of mind that prompts your parasympathetic nervous system to calm down the physiology of the "fight, flight, or freeze" response and return to balance. Mindful states of mind send signals to your body that slow down your breathing and your heart rate. They tell your parasympathetic nervous system that the danger has passed and it can bring the body back to balance. In the next section, you'll learn more about what mindfulness for stress and anxiety is and how you can practice mindfulness-based stress reduction to calm down your amygdala.

What Is Mindfulness?

Think of mindfulness for stress and anxiety as both an attitude toward living and a resilient brain skill that reduces your amygdala's reactivity. Jon Kabat-Zinn defined mindfulness practice as a way of paying attention purposefully and with nonjudgmental acceptance to your present-moment experience (1994). When you practice adopting the stance of mindfulness for anxiety and stress toward your own experience in the moment, whatever that may be, you open up the space to sit peacefully with and examine your thoughts, feelings, or body sensations, rather than following your amygdala's instructions to run away, be overwhelmed, or react impulsively. You replace fear of your own inner experience with a curious, gentle, welcoming attitude—free of judgment, self-blame, and aversion. Mindfulness techniques for anxiety and stress reduction allow you to remain grounded in the present moment even when you face difficult stressors, so that your stressful feelings and anxiety feel more manageable or less overwhelming.

Mindfulness for stress and anxiety is a state of mind, a deliberate, purposeful, focused way of looking at your experience in the present. Rather than experiencing stress or anxiety on automatic pilot, when you're mindful, you look at your feelings of stress and anxiety from an observer vantage point. With mindfulness practice, you're aware of the stress and anxiety flowing through your mind and body without feeling totally merged with it. You maintain the awareness that stress is a moving, dynamic state that's flowing through you but that it isn't all that you are. You're more than whatever's happening in your mind and body at the moment. Mindfulness meditation teachers often use the metaphor that you are the sky and your thoughts and feelings are clouds. The clouds float by, but the sky is always there. The sky provides the canvas for the clouds to float on. So you're the sky, and your feelings of stress and anxiety are the clouds. You can sit out the storm until the sky is clear!

The most common anchor used in teaching mindfulness techniques for stress and anxiety is your breath. When you get stressed or anxious, your breathing becomes faster and more shallow as your sympathetic nervous system readies your body for fighting or fleeing. When the stressful situation is over, your parasympathetic nervous system begins slowing your breath and heart rate to put the brakes on your stress response. With mindfulness exercises for anxiety and stress, you deliberately focus on your breath in a way that slows it down, even though this isn't the explicit goal—the goal is just to watch your breath. With mindfulness for anxiety and stress reduction, your breathing becomes slower and more rhythmic, which slows down your heart rate. The parts of your brain responsible for sensing movement and breathing send signals to your amygdala that the threat is over, and the whole system begins to calm down.

The best way to understand how your body reacts to mindfulness for stress and anxiety is to experience mindfulness-based stress reduction. The following mindfulness meditation technique will teach you to focus on your breath in a mindful way. The more often you do these sorts of mindfulness exercises for anxiety and stress, the more quickly you'll develop an attitude of mindfulness.

Exercise: A Simple Breath Awareness Meditation

Here are some instructions for a basic breath awareness mindfulness meditation. Do this once or twice a day for two weeks, and observe what happens. There's no right or wrong way to do this mindfulness practice for stress and anxiety. Try to accept whatever your individual experience is. The goal is not to achieve perfect focus on your breath, but rather to learn how your mind works! It's normal for your mind to wander, but when you catch your mind wandering and deliberately bring it back, you're learning to mindfully control the focus of your attention.

1. Pick a comfortable, quiet place where you won't be disturbed.

2. Sit with your spine upright on a cushion on the floor or a chair. If you use a chair, make sure your feet are touching the ground. Close your eyes, or maintain a soft, unfocused gaze.

3. Begin to notice your breathing. Try to maintain an open and curious attitude. Notice where your breath goes when it enters and leaves your body.

4. Don't try to force or change your breath in any way. It may change naturally as you observe it.

5. If your mind wanders, note what it's doing, and then gently bring your attention back to your breath.

6. Continue observing your breath for eight to ten minutes. At the end of the practice, notice how your mind and body feel, then slowly come back to the room.

As you continue this mindfulness practice for stress reduction for two weeks, notice if your mind resists the idea of change by creating judgmental thoughts such as I won't be able to keep it up or It won't do any good. You don't have to believe your judgmental thoughts; just notice them. Try to replace your judgmental attitude with one of curiosity, and keep an open mind so that you don't prematurely limit your experience.

In addition to paying attention in an open, nonjudgmental way, there are other characteristics of a mindful state of mind that create a powerful shift in brain functioning. In the next section, we'll discuss them in detail.

Characteristics of a Mindful State of Mind

Being mindful is more than meditating or focusing on your breath. Rather, it's a state of mind, characterized by the following attributes.

1. An Observing Stance

Mindfulness for anxiety and stress doesn't take away your stressful thoughts and feelings, but it changes your relationship to them. It's as if you're an observer who can look at these feelings without getting consumed by them or pushing them away. Thus, being mindful gives you more mental space and freedom. You don't have to be controlled by your stress response; you can redirect your focus, thereby gaining more control over your behavior when stressed.

2. Slowing Things Down

When your amygdala senses a stressor, it acts very quickly to "hijack" your brain for emergency action. However, not every stressor is an emergency, and successfully dealing with most stressors requires thinking of solutions, tolerating anxiety and uncertainty, and adapting to new situations. These are all functions of your prefrontal cortex, which is slower to receive and process information than your amygdala. Therefore, the first step in being mindful is to slow things down so that you can take a broader view of the situation before reacting.

Mindfulness for stress and anxiety moves your mind out of "acting" mode into "watching" mode, taking away the sense of urgency and giving your mind and body time to get back in sync.

3. Focusing on the Present Moment

When you practice mindfulness for anxiety and stress, you focus your attention deliberately and openly on what's happening in the present moment, both within you and around you. You may notice and describe your sensory experience — what you're seeing, hearing, feeling, or smelling right at that moment. Or you may focus on your breath to see what's happening inside and to ground yourself. This awareness of the present helps you stop ruminating about the past or worrying about the future.

4. Replacing Fear with Curiosity

Mindfulness for anxiety and stress replaces fear and emotional reactivity with an open, spacious curiosity. What's that thought or feeling that's arising? What does it look like and feel like? Is this something helpful or important that you want to focus on, or is it just an automatic event that you can observe as it passes through you? How does this emotion or experience change and unfold over time?

5. Openness and Non-judgment

Non-judgment is a key part of a mindfulness practice for stress and anxiety. When your amygdala triggers your stress response, you automatically begin to label the situation or your reactions as a threat that you need to escape. This is the aversion that the Buddha referred to as the second arrow. By observing your judging mind—a key mindfulness technique—you can avoid automatically buying into these negative judgments. You can then deliberately redirect your mind back to observing your thoughts and feelings with an open mind. This transforms your experience of stress by taking the terror and panic out of it.

6. An Attitude of Equanimity

Based on the Buddha's original teachings about non-attachment to pleasure or pain, a mindfulness attitude is one of peace, balance, and equanimity. To have equanimity means to let go of "needing" things to be a certain way. Equanimity keeps us from getting shot by that second arrow of addictive cravings or feelings of panic and desperation.

Everything is impermanent, everything is changing, and many important life outcomes are at least partially out of our control. Therefore, we need to stand firm and not be swept off balance by stress and anxiety.

7. "Being" Instead of "Doing"

When you're stressed, your amygdala creates an impetus for action to eliminate the threat so that you can be safe. Finding solutions or learning new skills in a stressful situation requires a goal-oriented mind-set. But your mind and body also need periods of rest and quiet so that you don't get depleted by too much "doing." Mindfulness for stress and anxiety teaches you how to just "be" in the moment, without any particular goal or outcome and without judging your experience or wanting to be rid of it.

In the next section, you'll learn to deliberately focus on your body or your sensory experience with mindful openness and curiosity.

The "How" of Mindfulness

It sometimes takes weeks or even months of practice to really understand what it means to be mindful. Following are different ways of practicing mindfulness for stress and anxiety. Try all of them, or find the one that works best for you. Research shows that practicing mindfulness for at least thirty minutes per day can actually shrink your amygdala (Hölzel et al. 2011).

Optimize your environment for practicing mindfulness for anxiety and stress. You may want to create a "meditation corner" with a comfortable pillow and some pleasant objects for you to focus on. A scented candle, a flower, or a smooth stone can be an anchor for your mindful attention, as I'll describe later in the book. Set aside a time every day for mindfulness practice, and put it in your schedule. You can practice mindfulness for stress and anxiety lying in bed, sitting cross-legged or in a chair, or even while walking, as you'll see below. Find the way that works for you. You don't always have to practice for thirty minutes. Studies show that five to twenty minutes of meditation per day for five weeks creates some of the same brain changes as longer periods of meditation (Moyer et al. 2011) I suggest you start with eight to ten minutes a day of formal practice and then gradually increase the length of your mindfulness meditations.

And so your mindfulness journey for stress reduction begins.

Exercise: Mindfulness of Your Breath

This mindfulness practice is the one I use most frequently with my clients because it allows you to really feel and connect with your breath and also to feel grounded and solid in your body. It's my adaptation (with permission) of a mindfulness practice used by Daniel Siegel, author of many books and courses on mindfulness and the brain. This version of the instructions is for when you sit upright on the couch. Feel free to adapt the wording if you're lying on the floor or bed.

1. Sit comfortably on the couch with an upright yet relaxed pose.

Now close your eyes or maintain a soft gaze. Let your mind and body begin to settle into the practice, noticing what your body feels like.

2. Focus your attention on your feet. Notice all the parts of your feet that are touching the floor. Notice your toes; where your toes join your foot; the middle of your foot; your heel; your ankle; the whole bottom of your foot; the inside and the outside.

3. Let your feet sink into the floor, noticing the support of the earth and feeling it ground you.

4. Begin to notice all the parts of your body that touch the couch— the back of your thighs, your seat, perhaps your back, your arms, and your hands. Let your hands and feet sink into the support of the couch and floor. Notice how your body feels as you sit, supported by the couch and floor.

5. Begin to notice your breath. Just breathe easily for a few breaths, noticing where your breath goes as you breathe in and as you breathe out. Notice the pause between your in-breath and your out-breath. If your mind wanders—as it probably will, because that's what minds do—just notice where it goes for an instant and then slowly, gently, direct your attention back to your breath.

Continue to do this as you begin to notice your breath in your nose, chest, and belly.

6. Slowly, bring your attention to your breath as it enters your nostrils. Notice whether it's hot or cold, light or heavy, and slow or fast. How does it feel? Notice where your breath touches your nostrils as you breathe in and as you breathe out. Continue to notice your breath in your nostrils for a few minutes.

7. Begin to notice your breath in your chest. Notice how your chest moves up and down with your breath like a wave, moving up as you breathe in and down as you breathe out. Just notice your chest as it expands and contracts with your breath. Watch the rhythmic wave in your chest as you breathe in and as you breathe out.

Continue watching your chest for a few minutes.

8. Direct your attention downward, toward your belly. You can put your hand on your belly to help you connect with the spot just below your belly button. This spot is at the very core and center of your body. Notice how your belly moves out when you breathe in and how it moves in when you

breathe out. There's no need to force or change your breath in any way. And if your mind wanders, bring it back to your belly kindly and gently. As you notice your breath in your belly, notice whether your breath changes or stays the same. Notice the rhythm of your breath in your belly.

9. As you notice your breath in your belly, begin to expand your attention outward toward your whole body. Begin to notice your whole body breathing as a single unit—breathing in and breathing out in a slow, steady rhythm. Notice the waves of breath as they move in and out of your body—filling your nose, the back of your throat, your chest, your ribcage, your belly, and your whole body with fresh, cleansing air. Notice how your breath travels through your body, and see whether it seems to open up any space in the area it touches. Just notice the rhythm of your whole body breathing as one: first the in-breath, then the pause between the breaths, and finally the out-breath. Breathing in and breathing out…

10. Slowly, begin to bring your attention back to the couch, to your hands and feet. Slowly open your eyes and begin to notice the room around you. Take

your time, and notice how your body feels now. Is there any difference from when you began the mindfulness practice?

When my clients do this mindfulness practice, many report a deep sense of peace, comfort, and calm. Feeling stressed can create tension, tightness, and constriction in your body, particularly in your chest and belly. This mindfulness-based stress-reduction practice can help open up space in these areas. A mindful focus creates distance from feelings of stress and generates a sense of peace and well-being.

Your breath is a powerful anchor for your attention, but this isn't the only way to practice mindfulness for anxiety and stress. You can also use your senses to create a sense of present-moment awareness and inner peace, as you'll see in the next mindfulness practice.

Exercise: Mindfulness of Your Senses

When your amygdala sounds the alarm bells, you lose touch with the present moment as your emergency response kicks in. You may feel compelled to "do something" about the stressor or to run away from the overwhelming feelings. By deliberately focusing attention on your senses instead, you move from a "doing," "getting," or "avoiding" mindset to "noticing and describing" what's around you. This mindfulness technique for stress reduction helps you feel more present and connected. We connect with the outside world through our senses. When we're mindful of what's around us, we gain awareness that we're part of a larger world of living and inanimate objects. Connecting with your senses can also be a way of what psychologist Rick Hanson (2009) calls taking in the good, or deliberately directing your brain to focus on relaxing or pleasant things in a way that helps calm down your stress response.

Walking in nature is a wonderful way to practice mindfulness of the senses. Being outdoors and close to nature has a calming influence on your brain and body, a natural backdrop for mindfulness meditation for anxiety. When you can't get outside, you can still practice mindfulness of your senses by adjusting the following practice to your situation. You can sit on your deck or in your garden or even look out the window, or you can look at pictures or photographs of nature scenes.

Exciting new research shows that walking outside in green spaces or even looking at nature scenes can increase your mind and body's resilience to stress. A study of college students (Bratman et al. 2015) showed that walking in green campus parkland reduced anxiety and worry more than walking in a busy street and had some cognitive benefits as well. In another study (Van den Berg et al. 2015), students were shown one of two types of pictures: either nature scenes, with trees and empty pathways, or urban scenes, with cars and people. They were then given a stressful math test. Those who had been shown pictures of trees had faster cardiovascular recovery (for example, their heart rate returned to normal more quickly after the test was over) than those who had viewed urban scenes. Measures of vagal tone showed that their parasympathetic nervous systems were better able to put the brakes on their "fight or flight" response. Benefits of mindfulness for stress reduction can occur whether the scene is one or three dimensional.

Mindfulness of Your Senses in Nature

As you walk or sit in nature, begin to notice your surroundings as a whole, noticing also how you feel in these surroundings. Notice that you're not alone —you're a part of the rhythm and pace of nature.

1. Bring your attention slowly to what you see. Notice the colors: the rich browns of the earth, the greens of the trees, or the blues of the sky or water. Are the colors bright or muted? Notice which ones draw your attention. Notice light and shadows, shapes and textures. Which surfaces are smooth, and which are uneven? Which are shiny, and which are dull? Which have sharp angles, and which are rounded? Just notice everything that you see. Now pay particular attention to one object—perhaps a tree or a flower— and notice its color, shape, and texture.

2. Focus on what you hear. Perhaps you hear the chirping of birds, the sound of the wind, or a babbling brook. Notice the sounds your feet make as they crunch on the gravel or sink into the earth. Do you hear people's voices? Do you hear a dog barking? Notice the pitch and rhythm of the sounds. Which ones draw you in? Notice how the sounds

emerge and then fade away—try to notice the silence between the sounds. Now pick one of these sounds to focus on. Notice its tone, pitch, and rhythm. Notice whether it stays the same or changes.

3. Notice what you smell. The smells around you may be sweet or spicy, earthy or fresh, faint or intense. Now pick just one smell to focus on— perhaps the breeze, the earth, or the flowers—and notice everything you can about it.

4. Notice what you feel. Notice the temperature of the air. Notice the feeling of the sun or the fresh breeze on your skin. Notice whether the air is moving fast or slow. Notice the feeling of the ground beneath your feet.

5. Notice how you feel inside your body. What's it like inside your chest, your back, and your belly? Do you feel any more spacious and calm than when you began this practice? Do you feel any part of you letting go of tension?

6. Notice how your feet feel as you walk. Try to slow the pace of your walking so that you notice each

step: Right foot up, moving forward, and then down. Left foot up, moving forward, and then down…

For a short version of this mindfulness practice for stress reduction, pay attention to just one sense.

For example, focus only on what you see, hear, smell, or feel. Or just notice each step you take as you walk, without focusing on your surroundings. You can also do this mindfulness practice for stress and anxiety just about anywhere, at any time—not just in nature.

Exercise: Mindfulness of Objects

Another mindfulness exercise to calm your stressed -out brain is to focus on what's around you. If you're feeling stressed or anxious while making a presentation, interviewing for a job, taking an exam, or getting ready for an important dinner party, try silently naming three objects in the room and describing their color, shape, and texture as a quick and easy way of moving your mind from "fight, flight, or freeze" mode to "notice and describe" mode.

At home, create a "mindfulness corner" where you keep objects with interesting colors, textures, smells, or sounds. Use it as a sanctuary when you feel stressed, or simply practice your mindfulness exercises for anxiety and stress reduction there daily.

Each time you visit your "mindfulness corner," spend a few minutes examining the sensory qualities of each object. Look at it, touch it, smell it, and taste it if appropriate. Things that might work well for this purpose include seashells, smooth stones, scented candles, mints, sprigs of lavender or rosemary, flowers or leaves, lemons, small glass bottles, wooden beads, soft fabric, and hand cream. You can also buy traditional meditation objects such as a mindfulness bell, a Tibetan singing bowl, a small statue of the Buddha, or a Himalayan salt candle.

The options are limited only by your budget!

The exercises in this book are great ways to learn and practice mindfulness for anxiety and stress. Yet, as we discussed earlier, mindfulness is also a state of mind and a way of living that's larger than any particular practice.

Practicing mindfulness teaches you a stress-proof attitude that you can integrate into every aspect of your daily life. And the more you integrate mindfulness or stress and anxiety into your life, the more opportunity you'll have to calm your amygdala when it starts trying to hijack your brain. In the following section, you'll learn some ways of making mindfulness part of your daily routine.

Integrating Mindfulness into Your Everyday Life

When you're feeling stressed or anxious, it's often because you have too much to do and too little time or because you're dealing with an emotionally difficult situation. Stress takes your mind away from the present moment as your amygdala focuses your attention on what will happen if you don't solve the problems or complete the tasks. Your mind may get tired and murky; you may find yourself getting distracted or zoning out instead of focusing on what's most important. You may run around on automatic pilot as your heart races and your breathing shortens in "fight, flight, or freeze" mode. These triggers serve to remind you to choose mindfulness to deal with stress and anxiety.

The following practice is adapted from a practice used by Dr. Elisha Goldstein (Goldstein 2010). Use it to become more mindful from the moment you wake up until you go to bed at night, constantly redirecting your brain back to the present and weakening your amygdala's power to take away your sense of peace and connection with the world.

Integrating Mindfulness into Your Daily Routine

When you first wake up, instead of jumping out of bed, make time for the STOP practice described here. It'll help you start your day off on a mindful note. Continue to use this mindfulness practice throughout the day whenever you begin to feel stressed or anxious, as a way of grounding yourself when stress begins to creep in.

1. Stop. Stop whatever you're doing, and bring your mind back to the present moment.

2. Take a breath. Take a few deep breaths to slow down your "fight, flight, or freeze" response.

3. Observe. Begin to notice what you're feeling, thinking, and doing.

What's going on in your body? Describe any bodily sensations (such as tightness in your throat or shoulders) you become aware of. Is there an emotion word you can use to describe these feelings (such as "angry" or "scared")? Try to stay in the moment with these feelings and "breathe into them": imagine sending your breath into the areas that feel tight, constricted, or activated by these feelings.

4. Proceed. When you're feeling sufficiently present and aware, go about your business in a deliberate way. You may want to simply continue what you were doing, but with a more mindful demeanor.

Here are some other ways to integrate mindfulness for anxiety and stress into your life as you get ready for and go about your day:

When you observe your morning routine, notice if your mind is already at work or school, worrying or planning how to deal with your daily tasks and challenges. When you notice your amygdala hijacking your thoughts, bring your attention back to the present moment. If you're in the shower, notice the flow, temperature, and sound of the water, the bubbles, and the smell of the soap. When you drink your morning coffee, notice the smell of the coffee beans, the warmth of the cup, and the taste of the first sip. As you eat your breakfast, slow down and pay attention to the sight, smell, and taste of the food and how it feels to chew and swallow. Mornings offer multiple opportunities to practice your mindfulness-based stress reduction skills.

Mindfully greet the other members of your household or your pets. Slow down and focus on what they're saying and their nonverbal expressions. Focus on your feelings of love for them.

Take time to say good-bye as you leave the house.

On your way to your destination, notice what your mind is doing. Try leaving the house a little earlier so that you can walk or drive more slowly. Let the things you would normally see as interruptions or obstacles (such as red lights or delays) be reminders to practice mindfulness for anxiety and stress reduction. If you feel yourself getting angry or impatient with the traffic or long red lights, direct your attention to your breath or focus on the things you see around you—the cars, the people walking by, the trees, the sky, and so on.

As you walk into work or school, drop off your children, or go about your errands, check in with your body and notice any tension.

Bring yourself back to the present moment by slowing down and focusing on your breathing, what you see around you, or the feelings in your feet as you walk. Do the STOP practice if you begin to notice bodily tension or negative emotions arising.

Practice STOP before checking your phone, checking your e-mail, or logging into social media. Set time limits for these tasks, and don't let them sway you into mindless reactivity that distracts you from what's most important.

Use STOP or breath awareness mindfulness practices throughout the day.

Notice if your muscles are tense, if your breathing is shallow, or if your mind is wandering. Notice if you're feeling reactive, spaced out, or focused and alert. Change your focus by moving or stretching for a few minutes, practicing mindful breathing, or getting some fresh air.

Mindfulness is a skill you learn through repeated practice. It represents a shift in perspective away from constant focus on stressors and amygdala-driven reactivity. It allows your mind and body to rest peacefully and enjoy the moment despite the stress. Stress can be there, but it doesn't have to consume you and take you away from the people you love, getting your work done, looking after your health, and being present in your life. But mindfulness for anxiety and stress is more than a change in attitude.

With a regular mindfulness practice for anxiety and stress reduction and by adopting a mindful attitude toward living, you can actually change the structure of your brain, as you'll see in the next section.

How Mindfulness Calms Down Your Amygdala

Researchers have been studying the effects of mindfulness on the brain and body for more than twenty-five years using sophisticated technologies such as functional magnetic resonance imaging (fMRI) to scan the brain in real time. They have measured effects of mindfulness on depression, anxiety, physiological responses, blood pressure, and resistance to illness. There's now a wide body of evidence showing that mindfulness meditation works to reduce your body and brain's response to stress, taking away some of your amygdala's power to steer you off course.

Mindfulness-based interventions are associated with improved mood, reduced anxiety, better coping when stressed, enhanced emotion regulation, and less physiological reactivity (such as sweating and rapid heartbeat) in response to stressors. A meta-analysis that pooled the results of twenty mindfulness studies concluded that "the consistent and relatively strong level of effect sizes across very different types of sample indicates that mindfulness training might enhance general features of coping with distress and disability in everyday life, as well as under more extraordinary conditions of serious disorder or stress" (Grossman et al. 2003, 39). This meta-analysis showed that mindfulness training reduced disability and improved mood and quality of life in people dealing with a variety of physical illnesses (such as cancer, chronic pain, and heart disease) and mental health issues. Mindfulness interventions have also been shown to reliably reduce anxiety, depression, and stress in healthy people (Chiesa and Serretti 2009; Khoury et al. 2013).

Studies show that mindfulness training for stress can make the amygdala less reactive to stressors. A study by researchers at the University Hospital Zurich (Lutz et al. 2014) focused on whether mindfulness training for anxiety and stress reduction could affect the brain when subjects viewed pictures designed to trigger emotions. One group of subjects was given mindfulness training, and the other group (the control group) wasn't. Then both groups were shown pictures while their brains were scanned. Subjects were given clues that indicated whether the next picture would be positive, negative, neutral, or unknown (meaning there was a fifty-fifty chance it could be positive or negative). The subjects in the mindfulness group were instructed to use their mindfulness skills (for example, noticing their reactions without judgment) when the clue indicated that an unpleasant or unknown picture was coming. The brain scans showed that, compared to the control group, subjects in the mindfulness group had less activity in the amygdala and in brain regions involved in negative emotion when they anticipated seeing negative or unknown pictures.

Repeated practice of mindfulness for anxiety and stress over weeks or months may even change the structure of your amygdala. In a study by Harvard Medical School researchers (Hölzel et al. 2011), an eight-week mindfulness course led not only to reduced stress and anxiety but also to changes in the brain: the amount of nerve cells and neural connections shrank in the amygdala but increased in the hippocampus. Neither of these brain changes was found in the control group.

Scientists have pooled data from more than twenty studies (Fox et al. 2014) to show that mindfulness for stress and anxiety reduction affects at least eight different brain areas associated with self-regulation, memory, focus, motivation, compassion, and resilience. In particular, mindfulness can strengthen your hippocampus, an area that has many cortisol receptors and can be damaged by chronic stress.

Your hippocampus can help you mentally process and file away stressful memories so that they're less likely to be triggered later. This suggests that mindfulness practices can make your brain more resilient to stress.

These research results are exciting, because they prove that you don't have to live in a monastery or on a mountaintop to calm your amygdala and strengthen your hippocampus with mindfulness-based stress reduction techniques.

Practicing mindfulness for stress over time makes your amygdala less reactive to negative events or uncertainty in your environment and helps your hippocampus process stressful events more effectively. In this chapter, you learned about mindfulness for anxiety and stress as both a practice and an approach to living that can help you better deal with stress.

Mindfulness meditation has its roots in ancient Buddhist philosophy, but it has been adapted for Western use. Being mindful means having an open, accepting, and compassionate attitude toward your own experience in the present moment, whatever that may be. It means allowing, rather than pushing away your inner experience; it means being in the moment, rather than constantly worrying or rushing around.

Mindfulness-based interventions have helped reduce people's feelings of stress, lower their blood pressure, and improve their resistance to illness. Mental health professionals use such mindfulness interventions to treat depression, anxiety, and substance abuse. Mindfulness has also been shown to shrink the amygdala (the brain's alarm center) and protect the hippocampus from being damaged by stress. The mindfulness exercises in this chapter can help you reduce your reactivity to stress and anxiety.

CHAPTER SEVEN

RECOVERY GUIDE TO ANXIETY DISORDERS

Getting rid of anxiety disorders isn't the same as taking out the trash. If you take your trash out to the curb, it's gone forever, and won't come back. But when you try to dispose of chronic anxiety, you often find that this task is more like the child's game, "Whack a Mole", than it's like taking out the trash. Each time you hit a mole, more moles pop up. Every effort that you make to fight against anxiety, invites more of it.

So you need to be able to work smart, not hard, to overcome anxiety disorders. This guide will help you do that.

The Anxiety Trick

The fears, phobias, and worry that you experience with chronic anxiety disorders often seem "irrational", and difficult to overcome. That's because there is a "Trick" to chronic anxiety problems. Have you ever wondered why fears and phobias seem like such difficult problems to solve? The reason is that chronic fears literally trick you into thinking and acting in ways that make the problem more chronic. You can't learn to float through anxiety disorders if you don't understand the Anxiety Trick.

The outcome of the Anxiety Trick is that people get fooled into trying to solve their anxiety problems with methods that can only make them worse. They get fooled into "putting out fires with gasoline".

The Key Fears of Anxiety Disorders

There are six principal anxiety disorders. The fears are different, but each one relies on the same Anxiety Trick, and draws upon the same kinds of anxiety symptoms.

And in each case, the person tries to extinguish the fears by responding in ways that actually make the problem worse and more chronic. Here are the key fears, and typical responses, of the six main anxiety disorders.

Panic Disorder and Agoraphobia

A person with Panic Disorder and Agoraphobia fears that a panic attack will disable him in some way - kill him, make him crazy, make him faint, and so on. In response, he often goes to great lengths to protect himself from a panic attack, by avoiding ordinary activities and locations; by carrying objects, like water bottles and cell phones, that he hopes will protect him; by trying to distract himself from the subject of panic; and numerous other strategies will ultimately make the problem more persistent and severe, rather than less.

The fear of driving is often a part of panic disorder.

If panic attacks and phobias are your principal anxiety concern, my Panic Attacks Workbook is a useful guide to recovery from these problems.

Social Anxiety Disorder (or Social Phobia)

A person with Social Phobia fears becoming so visibly and unreasonably afraid in front of other people that they will judge her as a weak, inadequate person, and no longer associate with her. In response, she often goes to great lengths to avoid social experiences, hoping that this avoidance will save her from embarrassment and public humiliation. However, her avoidance of social situations leads her to become more, rather than less, fearful of them, and also leads to social isolation.

The fear of public speaking, and the broader fear of stage fright are considered to be specific instances of Social Phobia.

Specific Phobia

A Specific Phobia is a pattern of excessive fear of some ordinary object, situation, or activity. A person with a fear of dogs, for instance, may fear that a dog will attack him; or he may be afraid that he will "lose his mind", or run into heavy traffic, on encountering a dog.

People with phobias usually try to avoid what they fear. Unfortunately, this often creates greater problems for them. Not only do they continue to fear the object, but the avoidance restricts their freedom to enjoy life as they would see fit.

A specific phobia is usually distinguished from Panic Disorder by its narrow focus. A person with a fear of flying who has no fear of other enclosed spaces would likely be considered to have a specific phobia. A person who fears airplanes, elevators, tunnels, and bridges is usually considered to have Panic Disorder or claustrophobia. However, the fear of public speaking is usually considered to be a part of Social Phobia.

A person with a Blood Phobia may fear a variety of situations, but they all involve the prospect of seeing blood. A person with a fear of vomiting (either fearing that they will vomit, or that that they'll see someone else vomit) would be considered to have Emetophobia. The official definitions of some of these disorders will change in 2013, so don't get preoccupied with the label.

Whether you have one or multiple phobias, these are very treatable conditions.

Obsessive Compulsive Disorder (OCD)

A person with Obsessive Compulsive Disorder experiences intrusive, unwelcome thoughts (called obsessions) which are so persistent and upsetting that he fears the thoughts might not stop.

In response, he tries to stop having those thoughts with a variety of efforts (called compulsions). Unfortunately, the compulsions usually become a severe, upsetting problem themselves.

For example, a man may have obsessive thoughts that he might pass swine flu on to his children, even though he doesn't have the flu himself, and wash his hands repetitively in an effort to get rid of that thought. Or a woman may have obsessive thoughts that she left the garage door open, and repeatedly check the garage all night in an effort to stop thinking that. Not only do these efforts fail to rid the person of the unwelcome thoughts, they become a new form of torment in that person's life.

Generalized Anxiety Disorder

A person with Generalized Anxiety Disorder worries repeatedly and continually about a wide variety of possible problems, and becomes so consumed by worry that she fears the worry will eventually kill her or drive her to a "nervous breakdown". In response, she often tries a wide variety of "thought control" methods she hopes will enable her to "stop thinking about it." Distraction is one such effort. Unfortunately, the effort to stop thinking about it actually makes the worrisome thoughts more persistent.

If persistent worry is a big part of your anxiety concerns, The Worry Trick is a useful guide to reducing the disruptive role worry plays in your life.

Post-Traumatic Stress Disorder (PTSD)

A person who has witnessed or experienced some dangerous or life threatening event (a shooting or a car crash) fears that the subsequent thoughts and powerful reminders of that event will lead to a loss of control or mental illness. The powerful symptoms of fear and upset a person experiences when recalling a terrible event are reactions to that event. However, the person gets tricked into responding to these reactions as if they were warnings of an upcoming danger, rather than reminders of a past one.

And Depression, too?

It's very common for people to experience depression in response to the way anxiety disorders have disrupted their lives. Less frequently, sometimes people experienced a strong depression before the anxiety set in, and this is a different kind of problem. Either way, depressive symptoms need to be addressed in recovery, so it's useful t

Exposure Therapy for Fears and Phobias

Exposure Therapy has been shown to be the most effective anxiety treatment for people with many anxiety disorders. You might already know that it involves practicing with what you fear, in order to become less afraid. But how does it work?

Exposure Therapy helps you retrain your brain. It's not just about "getting used to" the fear. It's about retraining your brain to stop sending the fear signal when there isn't any danger.

People struggle against anxiety attacks and phobias because they recognize that their fears are exaggerated and illogical. They try hard to talk themselves out of the fear.

But that doesn't help. So they end up trying to avoid the fear, and that, unfortunately, just strengthens it.

Exposure Therapy will help you retrain your brain to let go of phobias, anxiety attacks, and other forms of anxiety disorders.

Let's see how Exposure Therapy works.

Fight or Flight

When your brain gets a signal of danger, it triggers an immediate response, the familiar Fight or Flight response. That's a good thing, because when we face danger, we need to react quickly and powerfully.

Humans evolved in a different world than the one we inhabit today. It was a world full of predators, without police or deadbolt locks. Our main job was to get enough to eat each day without becoming food for somebody else. We needed a good emergency alert system to keep us out of the jaws of predators.

If we had relied on the thinking, intellectual part of our brain, called the cerebral cortex, to keep us safe, we'd be extinct. It's too slow. It's good for writing a speech, and figuring out your income tax, but not for making snap decisions about danger.

The part of your brain that handles these Fight or Flight responses is very different from the part of the brain you're most familiar with.

The Amygdala

The Amygdala, a little almond shaped part of your brain, is what makes these Fight or Flight decisions. The Amygdala works quickly, without your conscious awareness, because speed is vital in protecting against threats. You only find out what the Amydgala did when you feel its effects in your body (all the familiar panic sensations) and in your behavior (duck, run, escape).

Whenever we make a decision, there are two possible kinds of errors. One is a false positive. If you decide there's a tiger hiding in the tall grass, when there isn't one, that's a false positive. When you make a false positive error, you get afraid in the absence of danger, but you don't get eaten.

The second type is a false negative. If you decide there's no tiger hiding in the tall grass when there really is one, that's a false negative. When you make this false negative error, you feel okay, but you're gonna get eaten.

Your Amygdala doesn't care how many times it scares you unnecessarily. It just aims to keep you alive. It doesn't want to make any false negative mistakes.

If you experience phobias and anxiety attacks, and want to overcome them, you need a form of anxiety treatment which will retrain this part of your brain. The most direct and systematic way to do that is Exposure Therapy.

How Your Amygdala Works

Your Amygdala is always watching, passively, in the background, for some sign of danger. When it sees one, true or false, it presses the "fight or flight" button and fills you with fear. When the danger is real, that's a good thing. But your Amygdala works like it's still 27,000 B.C., and will often make the mistake of seeing danger when there's none.

It Learns by Association, not Reason or Logic

When you run away from whatever the apparent danger is, the Amygdala stands down and goes back to quietly watching. If you ran away from a mugger, that's a good thing. But if you ran away from a grocery store, or a dog on a leash, that's a bad thing. Now your Amygdala will be conditioned to see the grocery store or the dog as dangerous, and will make you afraid next time you see one.

The Amygdala learns by association. It associates the crowded store, or the dog, with danger. It doesn't learn by conscious thought. This is why you can't simply talk yourself out of a phobia or anxiety attack. The fear memory is stored as a conditioned fear, and can only be relieved by more conditioning, not discussion or reason.

It only Learns When You're Afraid

The Amygdala only learns when it's fully activated, when it spots something it considers dangerous. It only forms new memories and associations, new lessons, when you've become afraid. The rest of the time it's on autopilot, passively watching.

Do you see what this means? If you stay away from what you fear, your Amygdala will keep on "believing" the same old mistakes, without a chance to learn anything new.

How Can You "Talk" to Your Amygdala?

Your Amygdala only learns from experience. If you flee the scene every time you have an anxiety attack, your Amygdala learns that you should leave to be safe.

How can you get your Amygdala to learn something new? You have to activate it by exposing yourself to a trigger that gets you afraid. If you have a dog phobia, that would be a dog. If you have anxiety attacks on subways (or highways), you need a subway (or a highway). And you need to stay there with that fear until it gets a lot lower.

That gives your Amygdala the chance to learn that it got all worked up about nothing. That way, it can learn that dogs (or highways) aren't the threat that it had been conditioned to believe. And, with repetition, it will develop a new memory, one that lets you get on with your life without being disrupted by phobias and anxiety attacks.

Retraining Your Amygdala

That's how Exposure Therapy works. Exposure Therapy retrains your Amygdala.

You don't have to do this radically and quickly. What you need to do is to continually arrange to activate your Amygdala by exposing yourself to what you fear, and then stay in place, making sure that the fear leaves before you do. You can use a variety of coping steps to help you do that, or you can just "float", as Claire Weekes called it, and wait for the fear to subside. Either way, Exposure Therapy will enable you to retrain your Amygdala with new learning in ways it can absorb.

List of Tips

Tip One: Panic attacks: 13 tips to stop anxiety in its tracks

One in 10 people are believed to suffer from occasional panic attacks, often triggered by stressful events, while two in 100 UK people have panic disorder (recurring and regular panic attacks).

A panic attack is an episode of intense subjective fear, usually accompanied by symptoms such as trembling, sweating, heart palpitations and hyperventilating. So what can you do if you feel your panic rising?

Stand up tall

As soon as you feel a panic attack coming on, straighten your spine and stand or sit up straight. 'Not only does this trick you into feeling more powerful and in control, but it will also give you physically more space to breathe,' says Niels Eek , psychologist at personal development and mental wellbeing app Remente.

Get moving

Panic attacks can make our entire body seize up, responding to our perceived threat of danger. 'The best and most counter-intuitive thing to do is to start moving around,'. 'Do some stretches, go out for a walk, or simply walk around slowly.' Moving and exercise are found to instantly counter the effects of panic by reducing cortisol levels as well as lowering the risk of anxiety in the future.

Fiddle and fidget!

If movement isn't an option, for example if you are on a plane during take-off, try to distract yourself with a stress ball, some beads or even gum. 'Researchers at Tokyo Medical and Dental University found that repetitive and tactile motions distract the mind from the immediate feelings of panic'.

Splash yourself with water

Researchers in Japan found that cold water stimulates the parasympathetic system, which in turn slows down our heart rate, providing a calming effect. 'While you might finding the task of drinking water while you are panicking physically impossible, try splashing some on your face,' suggests Niels Eek.

Chew gum

A mental health study found that chewing gum for 14 days may improve levels of anxiety and mood. Chewing is known to reduce levels of the stress hormone cortisol found in the saliva. Fast chewing has been shown to have a more anxiety-busting effect than slow chewing.

Boost your magnesium

A study in the journal Neuropharmacology, found that low magnesium can make you anxious. 'Magnesium is the most important mineral for 'relaxing' nerves and muscles and is essential for the normal functioning of the nervous system, so is effective for panic attacks,' says nutritionist Shona Wilkinson.

Name your feelings one by one

Whenever you are in the middle of a panic attack, your brain struggles to focus on anything that isn't the immediate panic. 'However, if you start naming each feeling you experience, such as 'it's difficult to breathe' or 'I want to cry when this happens', it can help re-focus your brain and move away from the panic.

Try colouring in

Research has shown that focusing on a calming activity such as colouring in mandalas can help people with anxiety. It works by calming down the amygdala, the part of the brain that controls our fight or flight response and keeps some people in a state of worry, panic and hypervigilance, so if you feel the panic start to rise, start colouring. Findings from the study suggest that colouring in a reasonably complex geometric pattern may induce a calming meditative state.

Go herbal

Herbal remedies have proven to be beneficial in halting panic attacks. 'Herbs which may be helpful in reducing anxiety include Valerian, Passionflower and St John's Wort,' says nutritionist Shona Wilkinson. 'These herbs may be a non-drug way to help reduce anxiety and help bring about a more calm state of being.'

Carry medication with you

'Some people find that carrying some beta-blocker tablets with them can be helpful (these are non-addictive tablets which could be prescribed by a GP or psychiatrist), and they work to switch off the bodily feelings of anxiety, such as heart palpitations and tremors,' says Psychiatrist Dr Ian Drever. 'Often just by having these tablets with them, it's reassuring enough to stop many people having a panic attack in the first place.'

Remember panic passes

Dr Drever urges you to remember that no matter how bad a panic attack feels, it can never hurt you. 'It may feel like you're going to stop breathing, suffocate or have a heart attack, but these are all features of a rush of adrenaline, and they will fade away with time, leaving no lasting trace. Panic always passes.'

Create a soothing playlist

Listening to music can help to reduce stress levels and quash anxiety. Classical music is particularly effective at slowing pulse and heart rate, lower blood pressure and decreasing levels of stress hormones. But it doesn't have to be classical – some people find that creating a playlist of music around 60-80bpm can be a really effective panic-buster.

'This makes intuitive sense as this is the speed of a resting heartbeat. It also helps to provide an external focus rather than on an excessive internal focus on what the body is doing in the heat of an anxious moment,' says Dr Drever.

Bring on your panic symptoms

The majority of panic attacks are accompanied by physical symptoms, such as an increased heart rate, inability to breathe, dizziness and others. 'Focusing on the symptoms and letting them take over can often make you feel worse,' says Eek. 'Instead, try inducing the symptoms on their own, outside of the panic attack – you will find that you have no fear of them and that your mind will eventually get bored and move onto other things.'

These tips are something you can definitely try, but if you're having serious panic attacks then it's important to see a GP and/or a CBT-psychologist. Treatments for panic attacks are really efficient, and if the above tips aren't enough, can provide a real, working solution.

Tip Two: Quick ways to calm your nerves

It is tough to control psychological strain; stress is a natural response to tricky situations and the outside world. Some circumstances are simply beyond our control, making coping hard to do. Fortunately, you do have control over how you react to situations. Learning healthy responses to stressors is a great place to start. As compiled from calmclinic.com, Oprah, Prevention and Women's Health magazine, here's how you can regain your cool even quicker than you lost it.

Chew a stick of gum

Researchers from Australia and England found that in moments of stress and anxiety, gum chewers felt less anxious and had 18 per cent less of the stress hormone cortisol in their saliva. "Chewing increases blood flow to the brain, which may make us feel more alert, and it may also distract us from stressors," says study co-author Dr Andrew Scholey, director of the Centre for Human Psychopharmacology at Swinburne University. The study suggests that chewing gum can de-stress you in as little as 10 minutes.

Brew black tea

The study of black tea —instead of green or herbal varieties — found it helps cut levels of the stress hormone cortisol circulating in the blood stream. People who drank four servings of black tea a day for six weeks were able to de-stress faster and had lower levels of cortisol after a stressful event, according to a study from University College London. Chemical compounds in the antioxidant-packed beverage may relax us through their effect on neurotransmitters in the brain.

Try a tennis ball massage

The International Journal of Neuroscience reported that a 15-minute self massage twice weekly can lower stress by soothing the sympathetic nervous system. It is an effective alternative, as compared to popping beta blockers and anti-anxiety meds. "Simply rolling a tennis ball over tense muscles like the spine, thighs and foot with the palm of your hand can trigger a calming response," says Dr Tiffany Field, director of Touch Research Institute at the University of Miami, School of Medicine.

Put pen to paper

A 2010 study in Anxiety, Stress & Coping found that writing about a stressful event for just 20 minutes on two different days lowered levels of perceived stress. Putting feelings on paper appears to organise thoughts and helps process unpleasant experiences and release negative emotions. This is a good way to confront your emotions, especially if you're naturally inclined to write. If things become jumbled, just keep writing. It's the process of thinking and recording your conflicts that is most important.

Tune in to music

"The body's internal rhythms entrain to the external rhythms of music, like when you go to the sea, and you start breathing slower and your heart rate slows down and starts moving closer to the rhythm and pace of the ocean. It's the same with music," says Dr Frank Lipman, founder and director of Eleven-Eleven Wellness Centre. A study in the Journal of Advanced Nursing found that patients who listened to songs of their choice were less anxious and stressed. Boost your mood with clocking in at least 15 minutes of tune time daily.

Take a tech break

Before technology and smartphones, when you left your home or place of work, you most likely turned off the thoughts and emails related to it, too. Research shows we need mental breaks to refresh our minds and shut off the continuous stressors of work or classes. In a study by University of California, Irvine, and US Army researchers, heart rate monitors showed that checking e-mails and attending work calls put subjects on constant high alert with heart rates that indicated stress. "We found that shutting off e-mail eases anxiety," says study co-author Dr Gloria Mark. Commit to no e-mail or social media activity for 45 minutes a day to begin weaning yourself off.

Start Counting Everything

The next time you feel panic setting in, start counting your sensations. As Anna Borges suggested on BuzzFeed, "Count five things you can see, four you can touch, three you can hear, two you can smell, and one you can taste." This is another distraction technique that requires you to focus in on things that are real — like the sounds in the room, or the feeling of your shirt against your skin — instead of just the panic in your mind. It's also a good trick to use when you're cooped up on a plane, or stuck some place where skipping around and dancing might attract undue attention.

Clean the house

Housework's repetitive nature can help release tension and calm anxious nerves. "We get lost in the rhythm of folding clothes, mopping or vacuuming, which can disrupt stressful thought patterns and trigger the body's relaxation response," says Dr Herbert Benson, director emeritus of the Benson-Henry Institute for Mind Body Medicine at Massachusetts General Hospital. Studies have found that cleaning carries emotional benefits — catharsis, clarity, control and change. These good feelings lead directly to self-improvement and empowerment. Who thought doing the dishes could have benefits!

Just Kick Back & Accept It

Sometimes none of the above techniques work and you find yourself fruitlessly naming feelings, or pawing at a wad of Silly Putty. When that happens, all you can do is accept that the next ten minutes are going to be kind of sucky, and simply let the anxiety wash over you.

And often, that's really the best thing you can do. According to Gummer, "One of the most powerful things that you can do in the midst of a panic attack is to accept it ... Accept that it's there. Feel it completely ... Yes, it can get pretty nasty. But usually at the point when I feel like my whole being is going to explode from so much anxiety, something almost unimaginable happens: a release." That's because panic doesn't last long. It's important to remember that it'll be over soon, and that you will survive.

While panic attacks feel pretty awful, they aren't actually life threatening. So the next time you feel one coming on, try your hardest to channel the nervous energy elsewhere. In the best case scenario, you'll stop the panic in its tracks. In the worst case, you'll spend some time distracting yourself (and dancing around) until the panic fizzles out on its own. Either way, it will end, and you'll be able to go on with your day. I promise.

Tip Three: Anxiety Scams on the Internet

Anxiety scams abound on the Internet, with promises of quick cures for panic attacks, phobias, and other anxiety problems. When you feel desperate, when your daily life has been so disrupted by chronic anxiety that you're ready to try anything, it's very tempting to log on and buy the next product you see.

Maybe it will help. But there's a good chance that you won't get the promised results. The worse result then isn't even the money you spent, it's that you become less hopeful about ever solving the problem. So it's important to choose your self help tools carefully, and not just grab the first promise you see. Claire Weekes offered hope and help. All too often, anxiety scams offer hustle and hype. How can you tell the difference? How can you be an informed consumer of anxiety products? Most importantly, how can you find something that works?

Here are some tips;

Beware of quick, easy "cures"

Anxiety scams promise quick, easy results. They claim that the great majority of people who use it are "cured" of their anxiety. They suggest that the creators of the product have some special secret or insight which contains great power to help you, something that no one else has thought of. They often offer statistics which can't be verified, and testimonials from people who can't be located.

Anxiety disorders are solvable problems, and most people who struggle with them can overcome them. But recovery does take some work. If the promise sounds too good to be true, it's probably an anxiety scam.

Look for people with professional credentials

The Internet is full of programs created by people with no professional training in health care, psychology, or any relevant field. They're generally people whose skills are in marketing and advertising.

They often try to turn this to their advantage by pointing out that many physicians and therapists don't know very much about anxiety disorders. This is unfortunately true, but it doesn't mean that the answer is to turn to Internet marketers. The answer is to find better sources of professionally trained help, and materials written by people with the training and background to be helpful to you.

Be wary of affiliate programs

On the Internet, anxiety scams are usually marketed and sold through "affiliate programs". In an affiliate program, people with products to sell offer others the chance to sell the product through their own web site and keep a commission, typically 50-75% of the sale price.

It's quick, easy, and cheap to set up, and affiliates can make some money with little effort. Nobody has anything to lose...except the buyers. This is why you'll see hundreds of web sites for these products.

This marketing has become so organized that there's even a market for buying and selling the articles that affiliates use to promote these products. Affiliates themselves often don't know much about the product, and pay free lance writers to do the writing for them.

Check out these examples. Here's an ad seeking 9 articles on "fat loss, dog training, and anxiety attacks". How about this one - 25 articles needed, for which the buyer will pay $1.50 each, on the topics of "hemorrhoid care, learn spanish quick, and cures for panic attacks".

Everybody needs to make a living, but this isn't how I want to get my health care problems solved!

How can you tell if you're looking at a product sold by affiliates? Just google the name of the product. If google returns lots of web sites advertising the product, all fairly similar, and linking you back to the same site for purchase, that's an affiliate program you found.

Compare prices

Most of the best self-help books for anxiety disorders sell for less than $20. Anxiety products on the Internet are typically priced far higher than that, even though they're often only digital files which cost nothing to reproduce. These products usually range in cost from $60 to $100. The prices vary because they often offer a "special low price that expires today!"

You can buy a small shelf of books by Claire Weekes for less than what you would pay for one anxiety scam. Dr. Reid Wilson, Dr. David Burns, and Dr. Edmund Bourne all have written excellent self-help books which sell for less than $20.

When the price seems really inflated, odds are it's an anxiety scam.

Seek information, not just advertising

A good self-help site will freely offer actual information that you can use. It probably has products for sale as well, but that isn't its only purpose. It will offer actual self-help information about anxiety disorders, and give you a clear idea of how the products can help you. The typical anxiety scam web site consists of screen after screen of high pressure reasons to buy, and lots of extras if you buy NOW. However, they rarely describe how their product actually works, or give you anything you can use. They just urge you to buy.

If you read through an entire web site and still can't tell what method the author proposes for you to use, odds are you're looking at an anxiety scam.

See if it's available elsewhere

The Internet is a wonderful medium. But why aren't these products also sold in stores, and large outlets like amazon? It's often because the product isn't good enough to get approval from third parties like editors, publishers, and retail distributors.

If these products were sold in stores, they'd attract a lot more scrutiny. Reviews would appear in newspapers and magazines. Customers would thumb through the books on shelves. Some Internet marketers don't want this kind of attention. Their strategy relies on catching you when you feel needy - maybe when you can't sleep and you're desperately surfing the Internet for help - and get you to make that impulse buy when you're least prepared to make a careful, considered choice.

When you can only get it from one supplier, the odds go up that it's an anxiety scam.

I have so much trouble - isn't it worth a try?

It might be. These products are generally overpriced and over promised, but that doesn't mean there's never anything of value. You might get something out of it, even if it's only a placebo.

But it's not a good place to start. A better way to start might be to go to amazon.com and search for books about the problem you face. Read about the authors, read the reviews, and you can often read a sample of the work itself. The odds of getting useful help from books you find that way are much, much higher than just googling the topic.

If you do want to try out an Internet product, then investigate it as best you can, and take two more simple steps.

Don't buy groceries when you're hungry

If you've ever struggled to control your diet and your weight, you probably have heard this suggestion. Don't go to the grocery store when you're hungry and grab whatever appeals to you. Instead, make a shopping list when you're not hungry, and follow that plan when you go to the store. That way, you can shop in an organized manner, rather than impulsively.

Tip Four: The Anxiety Trick

The Anxiety Trick is behind most of the trouble people have with chronic anxiety. Have you struggled to overcome an anxiety disorder, only to get disappointing results, or even feel worse over time? You're being fooled by the Anxiety Trick.

This is a terribly common occurrence, and people mistakenly blame themselves for it. Here's a more accurate, and helpful, way to understand this common and frustrating problem.

What is an anxiety disorder? It's you getting tricked into feeling powerful fear in the absence of any danger.

It's because there's no danger that people seek help for these fears. People recognize that they're getting afraid when they're not in danger. If they were actually in danger, they would just protect themselves as best they could, and be better off for it.

With an anxiety disorder, people get afraid when they're not in danger. Their struggle to protect themselves from fear leads them down a path of increasing trouble. That's the anxiety trick.

How does this happen, that you feel fear in the absence of danger? This is the Anxiety Trick at work.

How You Get Tricked

* If you have Panic Disorder or Agoraphobia, you keep getting tricked into believing that you're about to die, go crazy, or lose control of yourself.

* If you have Social Phobia,you keep getting tricked into into believing that you're about to look so unreasonably nervous in front of people that you will be completely humiliated and be cast aside by your community.

* If you have a Specific Phobia, you keep getting tricked into believing that you're likely to be overcome by some external object (like an elevator) or animal, or by your fear of it.

* If you have OCD, you keep getting tricked into believing that you've set in motion a terrible calamity. You might fear that your neighborhood will burn because you left the stove on, or that your family will get poisoned because you mishandled the insecticide.

* If you have Generalized Anxiety Disorder, you keep getting tricked into believing that you're about to be driven mad by constant worrying.

In each case, the episode of fear passes without the expected catastrophe. You're none the worse for wear, except that you're more worried about the next episode. The details seem different, but it's the same anxiety trick.

What is the Anxiety Trick?

The Anxiety Trick is this: You experience Discomfort, and get fooled into treating it like Danger.

What do we do when we're in danger? We only have three things: Fight, Flight, and Freeze. If it looks weaker than me, I'll fight it. If it looks stronger than me, but slower, I'll run away. And if it looks stronger and faster than me, I'll freeze and hope it doesn't see so good. That's all we have for danger.

When people experience the fear of a panic attack, or a phobic encounter, or an obsessive thought, they instinctively treat it as a danger. They try to protect themselves, with some variation of Fight, Flight, or

Freeze.

How People Get Tricked

People's natural instincts to protect themselves are what lead them to get tricked. See if you recognize your responses in these examples below.

A person with Panic Disorder gets tricked into holding her breath and fleeing the store (highway, theater, or other locale), rather than shifting to Belly Breathing. and staying there until the feelings pass.

A person with Generalized Anxiety Disorder gets tricked into trying to stop the unwanted "what if?" thoughts, rather than accepting them and taking care of present business as thoughts come and go.

A person with Social Phobia gets tricked into avoiding the party, or hiding in the corner if he attends, rather than say hello to a stranger and see what happens.

A person with OCD gets tricked into repeatedly washing his hands, or returning home to check the stove, rather than accepting the intrusive thoughts of contamination and fire and returning his energies to the present activities at hand.

A person with a dog phobia gets tricked into avoiding the feelings by avoiding all dogs, rather than spending time with a dog until the feelings pass.

What Maintains the Anxiety Trick?

You might wonder, why don't people come to see this pattern, of repeated episodes of fear which don't lead to the feared outcome, and gradually lose their fear?

The answer is this. They took these protective steps, and there was no catastrophe. They tend to believe that these steps "saved" them from a catastrophe. This thought makes them worry more about "the next time". It convinces them that they are terribly vulnerable and must constantly protect themselves.

The actual reason they didn't experience a catastrophe is that such catastrophes are typically not part of a fear or phobia. These are anxiety disorders, not catastrophe disorders. People get through the experience because the experience isn't actually dangerous. But it's understandably hard for people to recognize that at the time. They're more likely to think they just had a "narrow escape". This leads them to redouble their protective steps.

It's the protective steps which actually maintain and strengthen the Anxiety Trick. If you think you just narrowly escaped a catastrophe because you had your cellular phone, or a water bottle; or because you went back and checked the stove seven times; or because you plugged in your iPod and distracted yourself with some music, then you're going to continue to feel vulnerable. And you're going to get more stuck in the habit of "protecting" yourself by these means.

This is how the problem gets embedded in your life. You think you're helping yourself, but you've actually been tricked into making it worse. That's how sneaky this Trick is.

This is why my patients so often say, "the harder I try, the worse it gets". If the harder you try, the worse it gets, then you should take another look at the methods you've been using. You've probably been tricked into trying to protect yourself against something that isn't dangerous, and this makes your fear worse over time.

How Can You Overcome The Anxiety Trick?

The thing that makes fears and phobias so persistent is that virtually anything you do to oppose, escape, or distract from the anxious feelings and thoughts will be turned against you, and make the anxiety a more persistent part of your life.

This is why people notice "the harder I try, the worse it gets". They're putting out fires with gasoline.

If you come to see that you've been putting out fires with gasoline, you may not have any idea what to do next. But the first step is always the same: put down the buckets. Stop throwing gasoline on that fire.

This is where the cognitive behavioral methods of desensitization and exposure come in. They're intended as methods by which you can practice with (not against) the symptoms, and become less sensitive to them. As you lose your fear of the symptoms, through this practice, that's when the symptoms will fade.

All too often, people get the idea that exposure means going to a place or situation where you're likely to get anxious, perhaps a highway or an elevator, and take a ride without getting anxious. That's not the point! The point is to actually go there and feel the anxiety, being sure to stay there and letting the anxiety leave first. This is what Claire Weekes called floating.

The way to disarm the Anxiety Trick is to increasingly spend time with anxiety, to expose yourself to the thoughts and sensations, and allow them to subside over time.

What can you do to make the experience of exposure more tolerable? You can use the AWARE steps as a general guide for how to conduct yourself while doing exposure. Always keep in mind that exposure is practice with fear, and do nothing to oppose, avoid, or distract from the fear during exposure.

COGNITIVE BEHAVIORAL THERAPY FOR ANXIETY

By

Daniel Anderson

TABLE OF CONTENTS

INTRODUCTION... 178

WHAT IS COGNITIVE BEHAVIOURAL THERAPY...189

COGNITIVE BEHAVIOR THERAPY CRITICISM....... 205

GENERALIZED ANXIETY DISORDER (GAD)........... 221

SOCIAL ANXIETY DISORDER..................................... 237

OBSESSIVE-COMPULSIVE DISORDER...................... 250

PANIC DISORDER.. 265

POST TRAUMATIC STRESS DISORDER.................... 283

SPECIFIC PHOBIA.. 294

AGORAPHOBIA.. 310

DEPRESSION... 328

EXPOSURE THERAPY.. 340

CONCLUSION... 346

INTRODUCTION

Cognitive Behavioural Therapy or CBT is a psychotherapeutic approach used by therapists to help to promote positive change in people by addressing their thought patterns, feelings and behavioural issues. Difficulties with irrational thinking, dysfunctional thoughts and faulty learning are identified and then treated using CBT. Therapy can be conducted with individuals, groups or families and the goals of CBT are to restructure one's thoughts, perceptions and responses which facilitate changes in behaviors.

The earliest form of CBT was developed by an American Psychologist, Albert Ellis (1913-2007) in 1955, naming his approach Rational Emotive Behavioural Therapy (REBT). Ellis (right) is looked on as 'the grandfather of cognitive behavioural therapies' Ellis credits Alfred Korzybski (who developed the theory of general semantics, which in turn influenced NLP) and his book 'Science and Sanity' for starting him on the path of founding REBT.

In the 1960s an American Psychiatrist, Aaron T Beck, (below) developed another CBT approach called 'cognitive therapy' which was originally developed for depression but rapidly became a favorite model to study because of the positive results it achieved. CBT therapists believe that clinical depression is typically associated with negatively biased thinking and irrational thoughts. CBT is now used to provide treatment in all psychiatric disorders and also increases medication compliance, resulting in a better outcome in mental illness. A major aid in CBT is the ABC technique of irrational beliefs, the three steps are:

A is the Activating event, the event that leads to a negative thought.

B is the Beliefs, the client's belief around the event.

C is the Consequence, the dysfunctional behavior that ensued from the thoughts and feelings originating from the event. An example would be: Susan is upset because she got a low mark in her math's test, the Activating event A is that she failed her test, the Belief, B is that she must have good grades or she is worthless, the Consequence C is that Susan feels depressed. In the above example, the therapist would help Susan identify her irrational beliefs and challenge the negative thoughts based on the evidence from her experience and then reframe it, meaning, to re-interpret it in a more realistic light. Another very useful aid in CBT is to help a client identify with the ten distorted thinking patterns:

1 All or nothing thinking - seeing things in black or white, if your performance falls short of perfect, you

see yourself as a total failure.

2 Overgeneralization - seeing a single negative event as a never ending pattern of defeat.

3 Mental Filter - you pick out a single negative defeat and dwell on it so as your vision of reality becomes darkened.

4 Disqualifying the positive - you dismiss positive experiences by insisting that they 'don't count' maintaining a negative belief.

5 Jumping to conclusions - you make a negative interpretation even though there are no definite facts that convincingly support your conclusion, this includes 'mind reading' and 'fortune telling' or 'assuming.

6 Magnification (Catastrophising) minimization - exaggerating things or minimizing things, this is also called the 'binocular trick'.

7 Emotional reasoning - assuming that your negative emotions reflect the way things really are, 'I feel it, therefore, it must be true'.

8 Should statements - 'shoulds', 'musts' and 'oughts' are offenders.

9 Labeling and mislabeling - instead of describing your error, you attach a negative label to it, i.e. 'I'm a

loser'.

10 Personalization - you see yourself as the cause of some negative external event which in fact you were not responsible for.

These are just some of the techniques used in CBT, others are, relaxation techniques, communication skills training, assertiveness training, social skills training and giving the client homework assignments.

Cognitive behavior therapy is a discipline of psychology that seeks to help people cope with dysfunctional emotions. Unlike other types of open-ended therapy, cognitive behavior therapy is goal-oriented and systematic. This type of therapy is often used for mood disorders, anxiety disorders, psychotic disorders, substance abuse and eating disorders. In addition, the therapy has been proven effective for some of the population in treating post-traumatic stress disorder, OCD, depression and even specific disorders like bulimia nervosa.

Because of the efficacy of CBT, it is often times a very brief experience, unlike some other forms of therapy that can go on for months on end. CBT may be individually based or based inside of a group. Recently, more effort has been made to use CBT for reforming criminals in correctional settings. In these instances, therapists attempt to reeducate criminal offenders on cognitive skills and coping mechanisms that will help reduce criminal behavior.

In this process, therapists/doctors will be identifying and monitoring a patient's thoughts and beliefs. (These will be discernible through a series of tests) The goal is to determine how these beliefs are related to the debilitating behavior, such as alcohol abuse, criminal behavior or so on. Cognitive behavior therapy was created in the 1960s in an effort to merge the best of behavioral therapy results with that of cognitive therapy. While these two disciplines had very different origins, they found common ground when focusing on treatment.

Cognitive behavior therapy has been used to help patients who are suffering from depression, anxieties, addictions and all sorts of other psycho social problems.

When undergoing cognitive behavior therapy a professional helps the suffering person to readjust his or her thinking. It is believed that thinking patterns and the way a person may perceive or relate to certain situations are connected with the patient's emotions and behavior.

Cognitive behavior therapy is a way to help find the underlying causes of the problem from a psychological point of view and then change or correct the thinking pattern that has led to wrong behavior.

Using cognitive behavior therapy, a professional is trying to modify the unrealistic and distorted thinking of the patient. This in turn will help the patient to make changes in behavior and to be able to re-adjust. Thinking patterns and emotions play a key role in human behavior and can be changed or modified.

Cognitive behavior therapy is also used to help people with drug addictions such as cocaine. In the strictest sense of the word, people who turn to drugs, both legal prescription drugs that are addicting, as well as illegal drugs, can be said to have a behavior disorder and can benefit from cognitive behavior therapy.

There are an increasing number of people who are suffering from dysfunctional disorders and while some believe medical treatments may be enough. Studies seem to indicate that cognitive behavior therapy is successful. Of course, a lot depends on the person's willingness to comply with a trained therapist and to modify inner thoughts and feelings.

The trained therapist also is helping the patient to understand past experiences and situations, to analyze and to learn not to react in an irrational or distorted way.

Cognitive behavior therapy has become a way of understanding the connection between inner thoughts and perceptions and human behavior. This no doubt has contributed to some success that has been made. It also has helped some people to make big changes in their life.

If you are a person who is suffering from anxiety or depression or any other kind of psycho-social problem, take courage and find a trained therapist in cognitive behavior therapy. You can learn to make changes in your life and help yourself and those who are close to you. Of course it may take you some time to see a difference in your life, but remember to accomplish anything worthwhile you need determination.

There are also many books written on this subject that you may want to check out. When going online you can also find tons of information that may help you to learn even more about cognitive behavior therapy.

The time you may spend can make the difference. The good news is that, even if you feel overwhelmed and discouraged at times, there is help for you. There is also help in form of seminars that you can attend to learn more about cognitive behavior therapy and how it can help you. Taking time to look over the information available may be your very first step to recovery.

There is a permanent cure for the wide range of anxiety conditions, including panic disorder, obsessive compulsive disorder, post-traumatic stress disorder, generalized anxiety disorder, social anxiety disorder, and phobias. According to the National Institute For Mental Health (NIMH), anxiety disorders plague 40 million American adults ages 18 and older. As we mull over significance of that staggering number, let's have a look at the recommended method of treatment, one that's provided recovery for hundreds of thousands of sufferers.

Cognitive behavioral therapy is actually a merging of two distinct therapies, both of which trace their roots back to the 1950s and 1960s and their acceptance by the medical establishment to the 1970s and 1980s.

Cognitive therapy was developed during the 1960s by American psychiatrist Aaron T. Beck. Beck originally applied his approach to matters of depression, then expanded his practice to include anxiety disorders. How it is that people interpret their daily lives and assign meaning is a process called cognition. Beck, disillusioned with traditional psychotherapeutic delving in to the subconscious, concluded that cognition, what his patients perceived, was the key to effective therapy that would lead to reliable recovery.

When developing his therapy, Beck first observed that depressed people adopt a negative perception of the world during formative years based on the loss of a loved one, peer rejection, criticism by authority figures, depressed attitudes present in significant others, plus a host of random negative events. Most often, this negative perception is fed and nurtured by a biased, emotional view of the world for example, all -or-nothing thinking, over-generalization, and selective perceptions that exclude vital, meaningful information. Cognitive therapy postulates that distortions in a person's perspectives grow into disorders. It is the job of a cognitive therapist to point out these distortions and encourage change in a sufferer's attitude.

Behavior therapy made its debut back in 1953, in the United States, in a research project headed by B.F. Skinner. In South Africa, Joseph Wolpe and his research group is credited with pioneering work. In the United Kingdom, Hans Eysenck contributed to the development of this type of therapy.

Behavior therapy relies primarily on functional analysis. Behavioral therapists have successfully been used as a treatment for intimacy problems, chronic pain, stress, anorexia, chronic distress, substance abuse, clinical depression and anxiety.

Behavior therapy is data-driven and contextual, concentrating on the environment and its context. Primarily, behavior therapy is concerned with the effect or consequence of a behavior, Behavior is viewed as statistically predictable, A person is treated as a whole, without the distractions of a mind versus body approach, but relationships, bidirectional interactions, are well taken into account.

Originally, anxiety conditions were viewed as by products of chemical imbalances and/or genetic predispositions. As these notions were abandoned, learned behaviors were credited as the source of most anxiety conditions. Hope for a permanent cure emerged, and, in the 1990s, cognitive therapy and behavioral therapy merged into cognitive behavioral therapy (CBT). The common ground for these two therapies is emphasis on the "here and now" by focusing on alleviating symptoms and replacing harmful, self-destructive behavior with beneficial beliefs and attitudes.

In the United Kingdom, the National Institute for Health and Clinical Excellence recommends CBT as preferred treatment for mental health difficulties such as OCD, post-traumatic stress disorder, bulimia, clinical depression, and even for the neurological condition chronic fatigue syndrome. In the United States, in spite of our obsession with pharmaceutical solutions, CBT has received acceptance within the medical establishment. Skilled, results-driven help is available for sufferers who seek it.

WHAT IS COGNITIVE BEHAVIOURAL THERAPY

CBT is a structured, action-oriented type of psychological treatment that was created in the 1960s by Dr. Aaron Beck, founder of the Beck Institute for Cognitive Behavior Therapy. In recent years, a growing number of clinicians are adopting this technique to teach people to "reset" their thoughts and reactions.

Nina F. Rifkind, LCSW, ACS, an Anxiety, Phobia, and OCD Specialist and Owner of Wellspring Counseling in New Jersey, specializes in using structured CBT. She knows from her own experiences working with patients just how powerful CBT can be. "CBT is an approach that focuses on identifying and restructuring negative patterns of thought and behavior that can cause distress and perpetuate anxiety and depression," Rifkind says.

Cognitive Behavioral Therapy (CBT) is a practical and widely used method to effect changes in your life and is used by psychotherapists, psychologists, and even some life coaches. It is a practical behavioral therapy used for many mental health and behavioral challenges including depression, anxiety and phobias. CBT is a modality that helps you change the way you think, the way you feel, and consequently, the way you behave.

Cognitive Behavioral Therapy can be broken down into its three components. First, Cognitive Therapy is based on the concept that current conscious ways of thinking can create problematic outcomes both physically and emotionally. In Cognitive Therapy a therapist will help you analyze your current thought patterns to identify any false or unhelpful thoughts and then strategize new ways of thinking to avoid these thoughts or choosing to think other more beneficial thoughts.

The second component of the CBT, Behavioral Therapy, is a therapeutic approach which helps you make choices about behaviors that are harmful, and find different ways of behaving that cause you less harm. There are different ways to encourage different behavior, such as exposure therapy, and mindfulness techniques.

CBT seeks to combine these two therapies through the practical understanding that often how we think reflects how we behave. If we tackle our unhelpful thinking, we can in turn, and at the same time, tackle our unhelpful behavior.

CBT is usually done in a structured treatment plan over many weeks or months. The length of the treatment is dependent on the severity of the condition and is usually a minimum of 10-15 sessions over the same number of weeks. Most sessions are just under an hour. Initial sessions are spent exploring the problem with your therapist, and the following sessions are implementing a practical strategy to deal with your thoughts, feelings, attitudes, ideas and behaviors around those things in your life that are causing you challenges. You will be asked during your sessions to take home "homework" which may take the form of journaling, insightful questions, and even short meditation processes.

Our conscious mind, or what we might call our cognitive processes, is what you think of when you think about your thinking mind! And as smart, rational and full of willpower as your conscious mind can be, sometimes this common sense and willpower just doesn't seem to be enough. Irrational fears are a good example of this challenge. Perhaps you have always been terrified of spiders. For someone with this deep-seated fear they would no doubt be more than a little distressed should you enter a room carrying a jar containing a large tarantula! Now both they and you know consciously, that a spider contained within a jar cannot cause them any harm, but anxiety and panic can easily override this common sense.

Because it is almost impossible to make change without both our subconscious and conscious mind pointing in the same direction, willpower, a tool of the conscious mind, is rarely sufficient unto itself. Cognitive Behavioral Therapy helps to support your willpower, particularly when used with other modalities such as, Psychotherapy, Emotional Freedom Technique (EFT- Tapping) and Clinical Hypnotherapy.

Who Should Use Cognitive Behavior Therapy?

The American Psychological Association's website says that CBT can be effective in addressing a range of disorders, including depression, anxiety disorders, alcohol or drug abuse, relationship issues, and other serious forms of mental illness. Rifkind also points out that CBT is appropriate to use with varying populations including children and adolescents, using age-appropriate language and explanations. Often CBT is used in conjunction with other behavioral health approaches; the treatment protocol is personalized for an individual's specific diagnosis and needs.

Looking at the Specifics of CBT

"Let's say an adolescent is having panic attacks in school. We need do our best to help the child identify the thoughts that trigger his or her physical symptoms of panic," Rifkind says. When a person is in the midst of a panic attack, adrenalin is rushing through the body, making it difficult to think clearly and logically. "Perhaps a child is afraid of being trapped in the classroom and feels dizzy and sweaty, and notices the heart and head are pounding," she says.

Once the child is not in that anxiety-provoking situation, then he can use CBT as a framework to challenge his fear of being trapped and to show that it isn't rational. "Once the person is outside of the situation, we need to challenge the catastrophic thinking by asking, 'Have you ever been trapped in the classroom before, and if so, did anything bad ever happen?'" The key in CBT is to counter catastrophic thinking with evidence of past experiences, and realistic probabilities, Rifkind stresses. She also points out that the behavioral part of CBT is to address the avoidant behavior. "We gradually reintroduce things [the person is afraid of] and pair them with new [more accurate] thoughts," she says.

The Components of Cognitive Behavior Therapy

People often experience thoughts or feelings that reinforce or compound faulty beliefs. Such beliefs can result in problematic behaviors that can affect numerous life areas, including family, romantic relationships, work, and academics.

For example, a person suffering from low self-esteem might experience negative thoughts about his or her own abilities or appearance. As a result of these negative thinking patterns, the individual might start avoiding social situations or pass up opportunities for advancement at work or at school.

In order to combat these destructive thoughts and behaviors, a cognitive-behavioral therapist begins by helping the client to identify the problematic beliefs. This stage, known as functional analysis, is important for learning how thoughts, feelings, and situations can contribute to maladaptive behaviors. The process can be difficult, especially for patients who struggle with introspection, but it can ultimately lead to self-discovery and insights that are an essential part of the treatment process.

The second part of cognitive behavior therapy focuses on the actual behaviors that are contributing to the problem. The client begins to learn and practice new skills that can then be put in to use in real-world situations. For example, a person suffering from drug addiction might start practicing new coping skills and rehearsing ways to avoid or deal with social situations that could potentially trigger a relapse.

In most cases, CBT is a gradual process that helps a person take incremental steps towards a behavior change. Someone suffering from social anxiety might start by simply imagining himself in an anxiety-provoking social situation.

Next, the client might start practicing conversations with friends, family, and acquaintances. By progressively working toward a larger goal, the process seems less daunting and the goals easier to achieve.

The Process of Cognitive Behavior Therapy

During the process of CBT, the therapist tends to take a very active role.

CBT is highly goal-oriented and focused, and the client and therapist work together as collaborators toward the mutually established goals.

The therapist will typically explain the process in detail and the client will often be given homework to complete between sessions.

Cognitive-behavior therapy can be effectively used as a short-term treatment centered on helping the client deal with a very specific problem.

Uses of Cognitive Behavior Therapy

Cognitive behavior therapy has been used to treat people suffering from a wide range of disorders, including:

- ✓ Anxiety

- ✓ Phobias

- ✓ Depression

- ✓ Addictions

✓ Eating disorders

✓ Panic attacks

✓ Anger

CBT is one of the most researched types of therapy, in part because treatment is focused on highly specific goals and results can be measured relatively easily.

Compared to psychoanalytic types of psychotherapy which encourage a more open-ended self-exploration, cognitive behavior therapy is often best-suited for clients who are more comfortable with a structured and focused approach in which the therapist often takes an instructional role. However, for CBT to be effective, the individual must be ready and willing to spend time and effort analyzing his or her thoughts and feelings. Such self-analysis and homework can be difficult, but it is a great way to learn more about how internal states impact outward behavior.

Cognitive behavior therapy is also well-suited for people looking for a short-term treatment option for certain types of emotional distress that does not necessarily involve psychotropic medication. One of the greatest benefits of cognitive-behavior therapy is that it helps clients develop coping skills that can be useful both now and in the future.

Setting Concrete Goals

Rifkind says she has patients who are afraid to leave the house, afraid to take the subway, afraid to have sleepovers, go to the movies, and a host of activities they may avoid because of anxiety. All of these, and so many other anxiety-based issues can and do respond to CBT.

For patients with anxiety disorders, Rifkind says she typically begins the therapeutic process by defining the individual's goal, which may be to drive long distances on the highway or attend a large social event. Then she constructs a hierarchy of steps to achieve that goal, beginning with the first step that the person is willing to try toward reaching the desired results. These steps make up "homework" that the patient completes in between sessions, repeating each step in the hierarchy until she feels comfortable moving to the next. "I also give people a scale to rate their level of distress as they begin exposure to their feared situation," she says. For example, if a patient is afraid to drive on the highway, Rifkind might ask her to drive for one exit and rate her level of discomfort. If the rating is an eight, the patient may repeat this one-exit drive twice a day until the distress level drops to a two, at which point she will increase her distance on the highway to two exits, and do the same when the distress level drops again.

"We build on these steps over time, as the patient gradually becomes desensitized to the fear, until she's able to accomplish her goals," Rifkind explains. Often, the issue that brings someone to treatment may not represent the entire spectrum of her anxiety. It may be a starting point, though, and once the patient tackles this, then CBT may be adapted to address other issues over time. Regardless of the specific issue being treated, the tools built with CBT may be applied to a wide range of circumstances, helping patients use these skills to cope in many situations. "Once people begin to see that the treatment works, it builds their confidence and motivates them to push themselves further toward their goals," she says.

Principles of Cognitive Behavior Therapy

Although therapy must be tailored to the individual, there are, nevertheless, certain principles that underlie cognitive behavior therapy for all patients. I will use a depressed patient, "Sally," to illustrate these central tenets and to demonstrate how to use cognitive theory to understand patients' difficulties and how to use this understanding to plan treatment and conduct therapy sessions.

Sally was an 18-year-old single female when she sought treatment with me during her second semester of college. She had been feeling quite depressed and anxious for the previous 4 months and was having difficulty with her daily activities. She met criteria for a major depressive episode of moderate severity according to DSM-IV-TR (the Diagnostic and Statistical Manual of Mental Disorders, Fourth Edition, Text Revision; American Psychiatric Association, 2000). The basic principles of cognitive behavior therapy are as follows:

Principle No. 1: Cognitive behavior therapy is based on an ever-evolving formulation of patients' problems and an individual conceptualization of each patient in cognitive terms. I consider Sally's difficulties in three time frames. From the beginning, I identify her current thinking that contributes to her feelings of sadness ("I'm a failure, I can't do anything right, I'll never be happy"), and her problematic behaviors (isolating herself, spending a great deal of unproductive time in her room, avoiding asking for help). These problematic behaviors both flow from and in turn reinforce Sally's dysfunctional thinking.

Second, I identify precipitating factors that influenced Sally's perceptions at the onset of her depression (e.g., being away from home for the first time and struggling in her studies contributed to her belief that she was incompetent).

Third, I hypothesize about key developmental events and her enduring patterns of interpreting these events that may have predisposed her to depression (e.g., Sally has had a lifelong tendency to attribute personal strengths and achievement to luck, but views her weaknesses as a reflection of her "true" self).

I base my conceptualization of Sally on the cognitive formulation of depression and on the data Sally provides at the evaluation session. I continue to refine this conceptualization at each session as I obtain more data. At strategic points, I share the conceptualization with Sally to ensure that it "rings true" to her. Moreover, throughout therapy I help Sally view her experience through the cognitive model. She learns, for example, to identify the thoughts associated with her distressing affect and to evaluate and formulate more adaptive responses to her thinking. Doing so improves how she feels and often leads to her behaving in a more functional way.

Principle No. 2: Cognitive behavior therapy requires a sound therapeutic alliance. Sally, like many patients with uncomplicated depression and anxiety disorders, has little difficulty trusting and working with me. I strive to demonstrate all the basic ingredients necessary in a counseling situation: warmth, empathy, caring, genuine regard, and competence. I show my regard for Sally by making empathic statements, listening closely and carefully, and accurately summarizing her thoughts and feelings. I point out her small and larger successes and maintain a realistically optimistic and upbeat outlook. I also ask Sally for feedback at the end of each session to ensure that she feels understood and positive about the session.

Principle No. 3: Cognitive behavior therapy emphasizes collaboration and active participation. I encourage Sally to view therapy as teamwork; together we decide what to work on each session, how often we should meet, and what Sally can do between sessions for therapy homework. At first, I am more active in suggesting a direction for therapy sessions and in summarizing what we've discussed during a session. As Sally becomes less depressed and more socialized into treatment, I encourage her to become increasingly active in the therapy session: deciding which problems to talk about, identifying the distortions in her thinking, summarizing important points, and devising homework assignments.

Principle No. 4: Cognitive behavior therapy is goal oriented and problem focused. I ask Sally in our first session to enumerate her problems and set specific goals so both she and I have a shared understanding of what she is working toward. For example, Sally mentions in the evaluation session that she feels isolated. With my guidance, Sally states a goal in behavioral terms: to initiate new friendships and spend more time with current friends. Later, when discussing how to improve her day-to-day routine, I help her evaluate and respond to thoughts that interfere with her goal, such as: My friends won't want to hang out with me. I'm too tired to go out with them. First, I help Sally evaluate the validity of her thoughts through an examination of the evidence. Then Sally is willing to test the thoughts more directly through behavioral experiments in which she initiates plans with friends. Once she recognizes and corrects the distortion in her thinking, Sally is able to benefit from straightforward problem solving to decrease her isolation.

Principle No. 5: Cognitive behavior therapy initially emphasizes the present. The treatment of most patients involves a strong focus on current problems and on specific situations that are distressing to them. Sally begins to feel better once she is able to respond to her negative thinking and take steps to improve her life. Therapy starts with an examination of here-and-now problems, regardless of diagnosis. Attention shifts to the past in two circumstances: One, when patients express a strong preference to do so, and a failure to do so could endanger the therapeutic alliance. Two, when patients get "stuck" in their dysfunctional thinking, and an understanding of the childhood roots of their beliefs can potentially help them modify their rigid ideas. ("Well, no wonder you still believe you're incompetent. Can you see how almost any child—who had the same experiences as you—would grow up believing she was incompetent, and yet it might not be true, or certainly not completely true?")

For example, I briefly turn to the past midway through treatment to help Sally identify a set of beliefs she learned as a child: "If I achieve highly, it means I'm worthwhile," and "If I don't achieve highly, it means I'm a failure." I help her evaluate the validity of these beliefs both in the past and present. Doing so leads Sally, in part, to develop more functional and more reasonable beliefs. If Sally had had a personality disorder, I would have spent proportionally more time discussing her developmental history and childhood origin of beliefs and coping behaviors.

Principle No. 6: Cognitive behavior therapy is educative, aims to teach the patient to be her own therapist, and emphasizes relapse prevention. In our first session I educate Sally about the nature and course of her disorder, about the process of cognitive behavior therapy, and about the cognitive model (i.e., how her thoughts influence her emotions and behavior). I not only help Sally set goals, identify and evaluate thoughts and beliefs, and plan behavioral change, but I also teach her how to do so. At each session I ensure that Sally takes home therapy notes —important ideas she has learned—so she can benefit from her new understanding in the ensuing weeks and after treatment ends.

COGNITIVE BEHAVIOR THERAPY CRITICISM

People struggling to realize their potential or find inner peace often turn to psychotherapy. Yet they find themselves wandering without much guidance through a marketplace of mental-health offerings and claims, lacking the knowledge to distinguish good therapy from bad. More than 150 different psychotherapies are offered in the United States.

In this section, I present some insights concerning cognitive behavioral psychotherapy (CBT), which has become one of the most available forms of treatment. My intention here, as well, is to show important distinctions between CBT and the depth psychology that I practice, particularly as these distinctions apply to clinical depression. Cognitive therapy, which attempts to address "distorted thinking" by replacing it with rational thinking, originated more than 50 years ago. By the 1980's, it was merged with the techniques of behavioral therapy to become CBT. This therapy now is widely offered, perhaps in part because it's a simple, straightforward method for psychotherapists to learn and practice. It offers, as well, a limited, controlled expenditure for insurance companies. I look upon it as the fast food of mental health.

Cognitive therapy originated out of the work of Dr. Aaron Beck, a psychiatrist and psychoanalyst who became convinced in the late 1950's that depression was not being effectively treated by psychoanalysis. Psychoanalysts believed that depression was caused by anger or hostility toward the self (self-aggression). Unfortunately, these practitioners were insufficiently effective in their treatment of depression because they were addressing only the aggressive side, not the passive side, of the primary inner conflict that produces the malady.

Meanwhile, Beck was finding that his depressed patients, from what they told him of their night-time dreams, were not experiencing anger or hostility toward themselves but instead reported feelings of loss, defeat, deprivation, rejection, abandonment, and incompetence. The inner life of his depressed patients, Beck observed, reflected a profound sense of weakness and helplessness, not the hostile self-aggression that psychoanalysis had identified as the cause of their depression.

Beck concluded from this, as he wrote in a 2008 paper in the American Journal of Psychiatry, that the negativity in his depressed patients, meaning their negative thoughts about themselves and the world, was due to distorted thinking about themselves ("negative cognitions," as he called it). Their depression, he decided, was produced by "a systematic cognitive bias in information processing leading to selective attention to negative aspects of experiences, negative interpretations, and blocking of positive events and memories." He wrote that, based on clinical observations supported by research, depressed patients were allowing their cognitive processes to be "hijacked" by "highly charged dysfunctional attitudes or beliefs about themselves," leading to the symptoms of depression.

Commenting favorably on this "discovery," Jeffery A. Lieberman, a former president of the American Psychiatric Association, has written that Beck introduced "a radical revision of psychiatry's conception of depression—instead of characterizing depression as an anger disorder, he [Beck] characterized it as a cognitive disorder."

This is, as I see it, a flawed premise. Depression is neither an anger disorder nor a cognitive disorder. Rather, it is a passivity disorder. The disorder results largely from the depressed person's inner passivity, coupled with his or her complete unawareness of the existence and nature of this passivity. Inner passivity is a leftover emotional deposit from childhood years spent in relative states of helplessness and dependence. Because of it, the individual fails to protect himself or herself from irrational, hostile self-aggression.

Passivity in the Psyche

Psychoanalysis was partially correct in asserting that depression was caused by self-aggression. But psychoanalysts did not recognize (and still have not recognized) the part played by inner passivity. This inner passivity, which is present to some degree in everyone, causes people to be inwardly receptive to the self-aggression. (It also causes them to be passive and lacking in self-regulation in everyday situations.)* The self-aggression is almost always derogatory, cruel, and irrational. So why would a person absorb such harsh, unmerited aggression and take it seriously, especially considering how unfair and irrational it is? The answer is that the individual is inwardly passive.

Dr. Beck correctly observed that his patients, in their dreams, were experiencing loss, defeat, incompetence, and so on. (This itself was their direct experience of their inner passivity!) Yet he didn't see that this passivity was the clue for why the irrational self-aggression (which, as mentioned, was claimed by psychoanalysts to be the main source of depression) was being absorbed into the emotional life of the depressed patients. As I mentioned, their inner passivity (their emotional resonance with feelings of loss, defeat, weakness, incompetence, and so on) rendered them unable on an inner level to protect themselves from the harsh insinuations and accusations of self-aggression.

The harsh self-aggressive part (inner critic or superego) is the same primitive energy that prehistoric humans needed for survival. The aggressiveness has been muted somewhat by civilization, yet it has not been, by any means, entirely dispelled from our psyche. Self-aggression becomes problematic right from childhood when, in some measure, it's turned inward against the frail ego, as Freud famously stated. The child's weak musculature is unable to expend all of the considerable aggression outward into the environment, so it is turned inward against the self because it has to flow somewhere. Later, as adults, we do expend much of our aggressive energy outwards in the form of productive and creative sublimations, providing we're not too neurotic (too inwardly conflicted), in which case we turn much of it inward against our self.

Cognitive therapy doesn't recognize these inner forces. It is biased in favor of the ego or the mind, in that it claims incorrectly that the rational mind can consistently be expected to overrule irrational emotions. Many people identify, to some degree, with their mind, which is experienced as their conscious ego, and they are prone to believe that their ego is the master of the self. They believe themselves to be in possession of a mental operating system that, as they see it, is firmly anchored in rationality. It pleases the ego, which strives for a favorable self-image, to believe that it's in command of rationality and can thereby subdue the forces of irrationality. This impression of reality is also attractive to people because it helps to subdue the inner fear that arises through deep self-exploration.

Stubborn and resistant though it is, our conscious ego is, in this context, still just a minor troublemaker. As mentioned, the big troublemaker is inner passivity, which is an aspect of human nature located in our unconscious ego and constituting, in all likelihood, much of the intrinsic nature of the unconscious ego. Through inner passivity, we become entangled in conflict with self-aggression (the superego, in psychoanalytic language). Our unconscious ego is subordinate to the aggressive superego or inner critic, and it takes a very defensive, weak stand—it represents our best interests very badly—in its dealings with our inner critic. It is from this passive side that our psychological defenses, as well as our inward and outward defensiveness, arise.

The Primary Inner Conflict

In my view, this inner clash between the inner critic and inner passivity is the primary conflict in the human psyche. Often our passive side's defenses collapse and it capitulates to the aggressive side and accepts punishment—for example, in the forms of guilt, shame, and depression—for allegedly being guilty of weakness, shortcomings, or failures, as claimed in the irrational indictments that flow from the aggressive side.

These punishments themselves frequently serve as psychological defenses. Painful feelings of depression, for instance, become a defense when they are offered up as "proof" that the individual is not passively absorbing self-aggression. The defense might be presented accordingly: "I'm not willing to be harassed and condemned by my harsh inner critic. Look at how depressed I get. I don't like it! I don't want it one bit!" This defense covers up the individual's great inner transgression (the deadly flaw in human nature), namely the unconscious willingness to suffer, of which inner passivity is a prime facilitator. The depressed person has been beaten into submission by self-aggression, and he thereby accepts the inner condemnation and the "appropriate" punishment, often in the form of very bad feelings about himself. This person's "negative cognitions," as Beck called them, arise out of this inner conflict. So cognitive therapy, by focusing on negative cognitions and attempting to modify the nature of those thoughts, is only addressing the symptoms.

Dr. Beck found that his depressed patients did have unpleasant dreams with self-debasing content, but he couldn't establish that the dreams revealed, as some psychoanalysts had claimed, any specific wish to suffer. The data only supported the fact that depressed patients suffered. Why did his data-collecting fail to penetrate deeper into the psyche? Humankind's unrecognized willingness to suffer is exposed by human consciousness, one person at a time, by way of a learning encounter with one's own inner reality. A person has to see for himself through inner realization that he is making choices that recycle and replay old unresolved hurts and feelings of weakness. For Beck to have succeeded in his investigation, he would have had to leave behind his data-collection methodology and plunged, personally and existentially, into his own psyche. Psychoanalysts do attempt deep self-exploration as part of their training, but these attempts are not, in my view, adequate or complete.

In addition, standard research methodology hasn't uncovered the possibility of humankind's emotional attachment to suffering because everyone, including researchers, are loathe to recognize this human perversity or flaw in our nature. While recognizing it requires a breakthrough in consciousness, scientific methods can't even determine the constituents of consciousness. The willingness to suffer, the masochistic contaminant at the heart of human nature, is a bitter pill to swallow. It strikes the modern mind with the same shocking impact that Darwinian revelations had on 19th Century minds. Just the idea of inner conflict alone, independent of the willingness to suffer, has become a forbidden topic in much of modern academic psychology. When the possibility of humanity's willingness to suffer is presented publicly, some individuals or groups loudly protest that the victim is being blamed.

A Passive Capitulation

The unconscious wish to suffer does exist. In the context of clinical depression, it can be understood as a passive capitulation to the inner critic's aggressive bullying. This self-aggression can be registered consciously, unconsciously, or semi-consciously. The passive capitulation, in contrast, isn't usually conscious because it's so well hidden behind a variety of psychological defenses. Once the passive capitulation occurs, the individual, as mentioned, absorbs the aggressive bullying and begins to feel truly bad about himself, thereby producing depression. This depression is not likely to be alleviated long-term by rational thinking. To overcome the malady, one's inner conflict is brought into focus along with increasing insight concerning the role of inner passivity. In our psyche, we can't fix what we can't see.

Dr. Beck didn't see the passive aspect. In 1962, he tried once more to validate Freud's theory of depression. He reasoned that a depressed person who wants unconsciously to suffer should not be able to tolerate success. He set up an experiment, a card-sorting test, that predetermined whether a person would succeed or fail. "Contrary to what Freud might have predicted," Beck said, "it turned out that depressed persons who succeeded on initial tasks showed a rise in self-esteem and did better on subsequent tasks than even non-depressed people."

The self-esteem arises, however, as a defense mechanism. Beck didn't recognize the unconscious cover-up, the psychological defense, at play in this situation. The depressed person, as a defense, is going to claim that what he truly wants is success, not the weakness and passivity associated with failure. When success occurs, he is likely to feel elated. That elation in that moment has to do not so much with the success of a worthy achievement but with the success of the defense in the cause of self-deception: "I want success, not painful failure. Look at how good I feel when success happens." (Such a person is likely to collapse into an episode of depression whenever a defense fails to be effective, as often happens.) Beck had also overlooked libido and the pleasure principle, that aspect of the psyche that is often enlisted unconsciously to make one's "successful" defense feel especially good, thereby strengthening that defense.

I mentioned earlier that depression itself is used as a defense. Guilt and shame, commonly associated with depression, are, in addition to being painful byproducts of inner conflict, defenses as well. Again, the defense goes like this: "I'm not looking to passively absorb criticism and disapproval from my inner critic. Look at how guilty I feel (or how ashamed I am) about my weakness and my failures."

Claims of Success

CBT therapists claim to have a high success rate following ten or twelve sessions, although new findings from around the world are saying otherwise.** It is true, nonetheless, that many of their clients or patients say they feel better. Why is that? The therapy gives people a sense of hope. They have been told by experts that they have the knowledge and technique required to escape the miseries of depression (or other emotional and behavioral difficulties). As well, they have unknowingly temporarily "borrowed" the cognitive therapist's strong ego and certainty to bolster themselves. They feel empowered, which in such situations is a temporary antidote to the underlying passivity. In addition, most people have unconscious fears about the "bad news" that can arise from deeper psychological exploration, particularly any revelations concerning their unwitting indulgence in their own suffering. So they feel a temporary sense of relief when their deeper issues are not addressed. They can also be employing a defense against the underlying wish to suffer, which contends: "Yes, I do want positive feelings, not bad feelings about myself. Look at how good positive feelings and aspirations make me feel!" When we're uninformed, some of our "best thinking" goes into self-deception.

Beck cited an example that he claimed showed the effectiveness of his method. A depressed patient, a lawyer, believed his wife had trapped him into marriage and then "cemented" him in by having children. "We examined the evidence together and he came to realize he had not been trapped," Dr. Beck said. After a number of sessions, the man understood that he looked upon any infringement of his freedom as being trapped. According to Beck, the man then started seeing things more objectively.

This claim of success is overstated. The cognitive approach fails to recognize the underlying irrationality. It's true this client of Beck's was feeling trapped, and it's also true, as Beck said, that the man would likely interpret any infringement of his freedom as being trapped. But that feeling of being trapped is a powerful emotional attachment associated with inner passivity. It's more than just a cognitive problem. The man needs to become conscious of his inner conflict: on the surface, he wants to feel his freedom within his marriage, yet he's determined unconsciously, even compelled, to experience the weakness associated with inner passivity. Feeling trapped is a symptom of inner passivity, as would be the sense of being beholding or subordinate to his wife. He might be blocked from achieving greater intimacy with his wife because, through inner passivity, he feels that intimacy will swallow him up and that he will lose himself in it. The rationality that Beck provided his patient (to the effect that the patient misunderstood marital responsibilities and obligations as infringements upon his freedom) would most likely collapse under the emotional challenges the marriage presents. That's because the man has no real choice but to experience whatever is emotionally unresolved, in this case his inability to prevent himself (without assimilating insight from depth psychology) from drifting toward the passive side and experiencing his marriage in such negative terms. He would continue, in a variety of everyday challenges that would likely extend beyond his marriage, to "know himself" through that passivity.

Depressed individuals must see clearly their identification with inner passivity and, in a process that entails acquiring deep insight, start to break free of their unconscious willingness to suffer. This self-knowledge exposes what was previously unavailable to their intelligence.

Another Clinical Example

Here's an example involving one of my clients: A retired woman, who experienced daily distress and regular bouts of depression, recognized that she was mentally distracted with worrisome considerations and speculations. Her persistent "circular thinking" dwelled on the past and the future, and it generated mostly worry and stress. She knew she was happiest when her mind was quiet, when she was able to focus on practical chores and creative projects. Yet she couldn't quiet her mind. What could cognitive therapy have possibly done for her when too much cognition was the problem? If she tried to think rationally about the irrationality of every little worry she produced, she would likely to flip her mind into hyper-drive.

Working in my method, she began to feel much better as she understood that she had been producing a steady stream of random, circular thinking because doing so activated the underlying passivity with which she identified unconsciously and which she was unconsciously determined to experience. Her circular thinking, in being so futile and uncontrollable, produced a sense of weakness and a disconnect from self. She felt like a little cog in her own life, which is a direct symptom of inner passivity. That passive feeling, she said, had been with her since childhood, and she had always just taken it for granted. Now she was able to see it in clinical terms, and thereby to use her new self-knowledge and growing consciousness to shift away from it.

The powerful allure of the negative side, to state the problem in another way, constitutes the unconscious willingness to suffer. Like an inner demon, this dark side of human nature laughs at attempts to dislodge it with so-called right thinking. Deeper self-knowledge and the heightened consciousness it produces are highly effective in liberating depressed and other neurotic people from their miseries. This knowledge, in all its relative complexity, might appear to be beyond the assimilation capabilities of everyday people. But most people exposed to the knowledge, and willing over time to reflect upon it, reach a tipping point where self-awareness floods in with all the accompanying benefits.

Inner passivity is experienced internally in the psyche in relation to self-aggression as well as in relation to situations in everyday life. Inner passivity makes it more likely that people will feel overwhelmed by events and circumstances, victimized by misfortune, unable to flourish, mistreated in relationships, a target of injustices, unable to self-regulate, and intimidated by the assertiveness or aggression of others.

GENERALIZED ANXIETY DISORDER (GAD)

Generalized anxiety disorder (GAD) is one of the members of the anxiety disorders' family. The distinguishing feature of this disorder is that expression of anxiety is less focused in it. A person may experience anxiety for many things and events throughout the day. This anxiety or worry is uncontrollable for the person and causes impairment in his daily functioning. The worried person focuses on his anxiety and ignores other disputes of life that deteriorate his daily functioning. This excessive worry may cause feelings of fatigue, lack of concentration, irritation, sleep disturbances and muscular tension in the sufferer. The worst part of the story is that such persons become habitual of remaining in aroused physiological conditions. When they don't find any reason in the environment to feel anxious, they think about past, extract anxiety provoking thoughts, and become anxious to maintain their aroused condition.

This is the disorder which is more prevalent in females as compared to males. This can be developed during childhood and adolescents. Common view says that females are sensitive naturally, and take more stress on trivial things as compared to females so, they are at risk for developing Generalized Anxiety Disorder. Anxiety disorders are internalizing disorders in which a person is affected at personal level. Females are mostly affected by these disorders. In contrast, there are externalizing disorders (Attention Deficit Hyperactivity Disorder, Conduct Disorder) in which sufferer acts out in the environment and, people in surrounding are affected by sufferer's disorder. During puberty period, females develop problems like stress, anxiety, and depression which affect them internally.

There is a strong need to psycho educate people for clearing misconception about the disorder. Psychoeducation is a basic therapeutic entity in which clinicians give awareness regarding psychological issues. The motivation behind psychoeducation is that people will try to find solutions for their psychic problems when they will know and accept that they are suffering from any psychological problem. Mostly in under developed countries, where women face different stresses in routine, people consider their disorders as lame excuses to avoid house chores. So, there is the need to develop the understanding that their exhausted behaviors have psychological basis. There is also need to reduce children's exposure to stressful conditions during their childhood. Moreover, try to consult a psychologist as soon as you notice any change in the child's behavior. If management is not attained at early periods of the disorder, then disorder may hold roots in one's personality and, lead to anxious personality disorder. Children may not develop anxiety if they receive proper information regarding pubertal changes. Sometimes, children have biological predispositions for developing anxiety. In this case, healthy environment can reduce risk.

If a person suffers from constant worry over the diverse issues and activities, he is supposed to be suffering from Generalized ·Anxiety Disorder. The things they are worried about is unlikely to happen most of the time. They remain unnecessarily involved in those things. Being worried sometimes about something is common to every man. But when it is constant and comes between our daily activities and takes away all our peace of mind, it may be the warning sign of GAD. So persistent worrying, tension and nervousness always shroud the mind of the person suffering from this disorder.

The difference between normal worry and Generalized Anxiety Disorder lies in intensity. Normal worry doesn't hinder you performing daily activities. But, GAD drastically interrupts social life and makes you overburdened with worries and anxieties all the time. Normal worry can be controlled and overcome by you but uncontrollable worry takes you to GAD. Unlike normal worry, the sufferer becomes extremely stressful and upsetting and tends to anticipate the worst. The person with GDA experiences a number of emotional, behavioral and physical indications. Though this disorder sounds uncommon, it is a somewhat common predicament that affects almost 1 in 20 people. It is likely to take care of Generalized Anxiety Disorder that often consists of recognizing the basic causes and shifting the thought patterns of the person. What is important is to find out an expert therapist with lots of experience to have the best opportunity of overcoming the awful affliction before it afflicts so many of your neighborhood and other associates.

"Do the thing you are afraid to do and the death of fear is certain."

- Ralph Waldo Emerson

I wants to tackle the side-effects of panic attacks. Most people who experience frequent panic attacks describe a lingering background generalized anxiety that stays with them long after the panic attack is over. Panic attacks are not spontaneous, random experiences. They are rooted in an underlying general anxiety that acts as the feeding ground for them to occur. Some people claim the attacks come totally out of the blue, but in fact on closer examination the person is usually already feeling an above average level of generalized anxiety before the panic attack begins. It is this generalized anxiety that we are going to tackle in this chapter.

People describe the generalized anxiety like a knot in the stomach accompanied by recurring fearful thoughts. This condition is referred to as Generalized Anxiety Disorder or GAD. This generalized anxiety disorder is the breeding ground for future panic attacks, and it is important that it be addressed and eliminated so the individual can go about daily business unimpeded by the uncomfortable stress sensations.

If we create a scale of anxiety from 1 to 10, a full blown panic attack would register at 10 and total, blissful relaxation at 0.

In a typical day, the average person in a metropolitan area might have a stress/anxiety rating of somewhere between 4 and 5. In comparison, people who experience panic attacks would say they reach the top of the scale (9/10) during the panic attack and do not fully return to feeling normal for quite some time. What is of particular concern is the fact that a large percentage of people never fully return to normal levels. Many individuals who experience frequent panic attacks often report that they feel themselves to be in a constant state of generalized anxiety, floating between 6 and 7 almost everyday. They wake in the morning with the anxiety and go to bed with the same feeling of unease. It is almost as if their body is stuck on a permanent setting of high anxiety. This constant generalized anxiety makes them feel jumpy, irritable, and physically unwell. The body becomes tense and uncomfortable and the mind obsessed with the anxious sensations. This permanent tension in the mind and body leads to troublesome sensations such as

✓   Nausea

✓   Dizziness

✓   Exhaustion

✓   Vision problems

✓   Cramps

✓   Intrusive thoughts

Feelings of unreality and depression

This condition (Generalized Anxiety Disorder GAD) is frequently connected to the experience of panic attacks.

Generalized Anxiety Disorder If you have been diagnosed with generalized anxiety disorder, do not convince yourself that you have a clinical illness. You do not. This disorder does not mean that you have a physical or mental illness. Your brain is fine; your body is fine.

Generalized Anxiety Disorder - GAD Symptoms

Everyone has some anxiety, but if you have GAD or generalized anxiety disorder, fears and worries can be so pervasive that they make it almost impossible to relax and have a normal life. Often people with generalized anxiety disorder - GAD worry about things that have very little chance of happening. They can also feel anxious all day long for no apparent reason. Generalized anxiety disorder - GAD can also affect you physically. Some of the physical symptoms can be problems sleeping, muscle aches and pains and tired all the time. Generalized anxiety disorder - GAD is a treatable disorder, there are many things that can help.

Sam's story

Sam would worry about things from time to time, but it never really interfered with his life. Recently Sam has been feeling on edge all the time. He has been having feelings of dread and worries about the future. These worries have not just been sometimes, but most the time. Sam has noticed that he is falling behind in his work and cannot seem to concentrate. When he leaves work and goes home, the worries continue and he just cannot unwind. At night when Sam goes to bed he is having a hard time falling asleep. He is restless and cannot seem to fall asleep for hours. Sam also is having digestive upset, this includes diarrhea, intestinal and stomach cramps along with bloating. On top of all this Sam has been taking aspirin 4 - 5 times a day for his stiff muscles. He wonders how long he can keep going, he feels like he may be ready for a nervous breakdown.

If you are suffering from generalized anxiety disorder - GAD, it is very common to worry about the same things that other people worry about. The problem becomes, that these worries become overwhelming and often you can create scenarios that are very unlikely to happen. Things like a innocent mention of the stock market turns into the thought that all your investments will be worthless. Maybe you try to call your child and they do not answer, you then start thinking of all the worst possibilities. Even the thought of getting out of bed and going to work can cause anxiety. It does not matter if you think your anxiety is more intense than others or not, the problem is it will not go away, you are always worrying about something. Generalized anxiety disorder - GAD is worrying about things that are not related to each other in a way that would be considered excessive. This type of worry can make your life very difficult and being able to relax and unwind becomes almost impossible.

GAD And Normal Worry

It is perfectly normal to have fears, doubts and worries. It is understandable that you will be anxious about a big interview or going out on a first date. What make generalized anxiety disorder - GAD different is the fears, worries, doubts are disruptive in your life and are much more frequent then the average person. As an example, if the average person was watching the news and saw a report about a natural disaster overseas, they become a little worried about the situation. Someone with generalized anxiety disorder - GAD could spend the next several nights worried about something happening in their area. They may think about the worst possible thing that could happen. People with generalized anxiety disorder - GAD tend not to avoid work and social situations, but they are filled with anxiety as they move through their daily lives. This can be the case even though they have nothing of any significance to worry about. For some people the physical symptoms associated with generalized anxiety disorder - GAD make everyday functioning very difficult.

Examples of normal worry

✓ Your daily activities are not affected in a negative way by worrying.

✓ You can keep your worries under control.

✓ You do not experience high stress from your worries.

✓ You only worry about things that are realistic.

✓ You worry only for short periods.

✓ Examples of generalized anxiety disorder - GAD worry

✓ Your job, social life and daily activities are severely disrupted from worry.

✓ You cannot control the worry

✓ The worry tends to be very stressful and upsetting.

✓ When you worry you expect the worst.

✓ You worry everyday and this has been going on for over six months.

Symptoms Of Generalized Anxiety Disorder - Gad

Symptoms of generalized anxiety disorder - GAD can be different from day to day. At certain times of the day you may feel better than at other times of the day. You may also have some days that are better than other days. Stress will not cause generalized anxiety disorder - GAD, but it can make the problem worse. People with generalized anxiety disorder - GAD will not all have the same symptoms, but most people will have some combination of the following symptoms.

✓ Physical Symptoms can include.

✓ Muscle tension, aches, or soreness

✓ Trouble falling asleep or staying asleep

✓ Stomach problems, nausea, diarrhea

✓ Jumpiness or unsteadiness

✓ Edginess or restlessness

✓ Get tired easily

✓ Psychological symptoms can include

✓ Irritability

✓ Feelings of dread

✓ Cannot control anxious thoughts

✓ Cannot relax

✓ Having difficulty concentrating

✓ Afraid you will lose control or be rejected

Generalized Anxiety Disorder - GAD Help

Anxiety disorders, as a cluster, are the foremost common mental illness in America. Additionally over nineteen million adults in America are stricken by these debilitating sicknesses each year.

Youngsters and adolescents can conjointly develop anxiety.

Anxiety disorders, such as obsessive-compulsive disorder or panic attacks, are sicknesses that fill folks's lives with overwhelming worry and fear. These feelings are generally chronic, unremitting, and will grow progressively worse. It isn't uncommon for someone to have additional than one anxiety disorder.

Fortunately, treatments for the condition can be effective at any age.

Anxiety disorder is defined as constant, exaggerated worrisome thoughts and tension about everyday, routine life events and activities. These thoughts should last a minimum of six months to be classified as generalized anxiety disorder. Individuals with this condition almost forever anticipate the worst, even though there's very little reason to expect it. These feelings are in the midst of physical symptoms, like:

- ✓ Fatigue

- ✓ Trembling

- ✓ Muscle Tension

- ✓ Headache

- ✓ Nausea

✓ What Causes It?

Scientists aren't quite certain why some folks have this problem. Different individuals exposed to the same scenario can react in terribly totally different ways. Half of this distinction might be within the genes they have inherited.

Anxiety disorders run in families, thus if a parent has it the kids have a better likelihood of developing one of those conditions. This could be because of the genes they've inherited, however the surroundings a child is raised in could be necessary, too. Ultimately, it's probably an interaction between an individual's genetic predisposition and environment.

Scientists have recently been gaining insights into the event of anxiety disorders. Kids of oldsters with panic disorders have the next incidence of behavioral disorders terribly early in life, before you would think major environmental impacts would occur.

A growing body of evidence shows that infants who have a tendency to be keep, timid, and constrained in social things -- even in the first few weeks of life -- have higher rates of anxiety disorders when they get older.

Treatment Choices

Anxiety treatment will be effective at any age. If you think that you will have an anxiety disorder, don't hesitate to debate it with your healthcare provider.

There are many varieties of treatments out there, and these will be tailored to specific problems. In some cases, psychotherapy, or counseling, is sufficient. In alternative cases, medication alone will be effective. Some individuals could need both.

A range of medicines that were originally approved for treating depression are found to be effective for anxiety disorders as well. Some of the latest of these antidepressants are known as selective serotonin reuptake inhibitors (SSRIs). Alternative anti-anxiety medications embody teams of drugs known as benzodiazepines and beta-blockers. If one medication is not effective, others can be tried. New medications are currently underneath development to treat anxiety symptoms.

Two clinically proven effective types of psychotherapy used to treat anxiety disorders are behavioral therapy and cognitive-behavioral therapy. Behavioral therapy focuses on changing specific actions, and uses several techniques to stop unwanted behaviors. In addition to the behavioral therapy techniques, cognitive-behavioral therapy teaches patients to perceive and amendment their thinking patterns thus that they'll react differently to the situations that cause them anxiety.

Generalized Anxiety can be effectively treated and in most cases generalized anxiety can even be eliminated.

SOCIAL ANXIETY DISORDER

Social anxiety disorder, formerly referred to as social phobia, is an anxiety disorder characterized by overwhelming anxiety and excessive self-consciousness in everyday social situations. People with social anxiety disorder have a persistent, intense, and chronic fear of being watched and judged by others and of being embarrassed or humiliated by their own actions. Their fear may be so severe that it interferes with work, school, or other activities. While many people with social anxiety disorder recognize that their fear of being around people may be excessive or unreasonable, they are unable to overcome it. They often worry for days or weeks in advance of a dreaded situation. In addition, they often experience low self-esteem and depression.

Social anxiety disorder is identified as a feeling of extreme self-consciousness in public places. Sometimes overwhelming physical symptoms will accompany attacks of fear. A person with social anxiety disorder might not even feel comfortable about eating in public. They might be so afraid of embarrassing themselves, that they are overcome by a choking sensation while trying to eat.

Social anxiety disorder tends to affect different people in different ways, so a "one size fits all" approach cannot be applied here. Some people, for example, might only suffer from very situational problems. People with extreme fears of public speaking would fit into this category. Social anxiety disorder might prohibit others from speaking on the telephone, dating or attending parties. Other social situations however would not be a problem for these individuals, and they would be perfectly well able to cope.

In its worst form social anxiety disorder, can and does infiltrate all aspects of life. Someone with severe social anxiety disorder might dread going to school, going to work or leaving the safety of their own house to take in a movie, or go on a date. While all forms of social anxiety disorder have a detrimental effect on a person's ability to enjoy life to the fullest, those who suffer from extreme cases, withdraw from life almost completely.

Sometimes it is difficult to differentiate the normal social anxiety that every individual feels to some extent from this chronic condition. Everyone has some degree of social anxiety in them, yet when such anxiety becomes so overriding that the person starts avoiding all social interactions as a result of his anxiety and the physical symptoms cause him distress beyond natural parameters, it is clear that it is a result of this disorder. Most often close family members or friends can recognize this, since they have a better perspective of the patient's suffering.

Social anxiety disorder can be limited to only one type of situation—such as a fear of speaking or performing in public—or a person can experience symptoms whenever they are around other people. If left untreated, social phobia can have severe consequences. For example, it may keep people from going to work or school on some days. Many with this illness are afraid of being with people other than family members. As a result, they may have a hard time making and keeping friends.

Social anxiety disorder often runs in families and may be accompanied by depression or other anxiety disorders, such as panic disorder or obsessive-compulsive disorder. Some people with social anxiety disorder self-medicate with alcohol or other drugs, which can lead to addiction.

Prevalence of Social Phobia

About seven percent of the U.S. population is estimated to have social anxiety disorder within a given 12-month period. Social anxiety disorder occurs twice as often in women as in men, although a higher proportion of men seek help for this condition. The disorder typically begins in childhood or early adolescence and rarely develops after age 25.

Sandra's story

Sandra is a 35-year-old single woman who lives alone. She feels extremely uncomfortable interacting with other people, and worries that others think badly of her. She was extremely anxious as a child and spent most of her time alone because she had trouble making friends. Sandra's main fears are that other people will disagree with her and that she will say something to offend someone. She is very concerned that interacting with other people will lead to some kind of conflict that she will not be able to handle. As a result, she avoids conversations where she might have to give her personal opinions, and she finds it difficult to be assertive. She feels especially anxious around family members and people who live in her apartment building.

Sandra feels anxious for most of the day and finds her social fears quite distressing. She has been unemployed for the past 3 months. She left her job due to extreme anxiety when interacting with co-workers and customers. She would like to develop some friendships, but tends to avoid people because she fears that they won't like her once they get to know her. Recently, she has been using alcohol to try and reduce her anxiety at family functions. She feels that she is starting to become dependent on alcohol and worries that family members will confront her about her drinking.

Sandra wants to have a romantic relationship, as well as close relationships with friends and family, but she feels too tense and nervous to get close to others. She spends much of her time thinking about everything she is missing out on because of her fears. She is worried she will never be able to have a family of her own, and she is finding it harder and harder to be optimistic about her future

What Is A Social Situation?

A social situation includes any situation in which you and at least 1 other person are present. Social situations tend to fall into 2 main categories: performance situations and interpersonal interactions.

Performance Situations

Interpersonal Interactions

These are situations where people feel they are being observed by others. Examples include:

✓ Public speaking (e.g. presenting at a meeting

✓ Participating in meetings or classes (e.g. asking or answering questions)

✓ Eating in front of others

✓ Using public washrooms

✓ Writing in front of others (e.g. signing a cheque of filling out a form)

✓ Performing in public (e.g. singing or acting on stage, or playing a sport)

✓ Entering a room where everyone is already seated

These are situations where people are interacting with others and developing closer relationships. Examples include:

✓ Meeting new people

✓ Talking to co-workers or friends

✓ Inviting others to do things

✓ Going to social events (e.g. parties or dinners)

✓ Dating

✓ Being assertive

✓ Expressing opinions

✓ Talking on the phone

✓ Working in a group (e.g. working on a project with other co-workers)

✓ Ordering food at a restaurant

✓ Returning something at a store

✓ Having a job interview

Note:

It is not uncommon for people to fear some social situations and feel quite comfortable in others. For example, some people are comfortable spending time with friends and family, and interacting socially with co-workers but are very fearful of performance situations, such as participating in business meetings or giving formal speeches. Also, some people fear only a single situation (such as public speaking), while others fear and avoid a wide range of social situations.

Symptoms

A diagnosis of social anxiety disorder is made only if this avoidance, fear, or anxious anticipation of a social or performance situation interferes with daily routine, occupational functioning, and social life or if there is marked distress as a result of the anxiety. The Diagnostic and Statistical Manual of Mental Disorders (DSM-V) provides the following criteria for diagnosing social anxiety disorder:

The individual fears one or more social or performance situations in which he or she is exposed to possible scrutiny by others. Examples include meeting unfamiliar people, being observed eating or drinking, or giving a speech or other type of performance.

The individual fears behaving in a manner that causes embarrassment or being negatively evaluated in some way.

Exposure to social situations almost always causes intense anxiety.

The feared situation is avoided or endured with anxiety and distress.

The fear or anxiety is out of proportion to the actual threat posed by the social situation.

The fear or anxiety is persistent and typically lasts for six months or longer.

The avoidance, anxious anticipation, or distress interferes significantly with the person's social, academic, or occupational functioning.

Additionally, the diagnosis can specify whether the anxiety or fear is present only when the person is speaking or performing in public.

The physical symptoms of social anxiety disorder include the following:

Blushing, sweating, trembling, experiencing a rapid heart rate, or feeling the "mind going blank"

Nausea or upset stomach

Displaying a rigid body posture, poor eye contact, or speaking too quietly

Causes

While research to better understand the causes of social anxiety disorder is ongoing, some investigations implicate a small structure in the brain called the amygdala in the symptoms of social phobia. The amygdala is believed to be a central site in the brain that controls fear responses.

Social anxiety disorder is heritable. In fact, first-degree relatives have a two to six time's higher chance of developing social anxiety disorder. Research supported by the National Institute of Mental Health (NIMH) has also identified the site of a gene in mice that affects learned fearfulness. Scientists are exploring the idea that heightened sensitivity to disapproval may be physiologically or hormonally based. Other researchers are investigating the environment's influence on the development of social phobia. Childhood maltreatment and adversity are risk factors for social anxiety disorder.

Treatments

Most anxiety disorders can be treated successfully by a trained mental health care professional.

Research has shown that there are two main forms of effective treatment for social anxiety disorder: psychotherapy and certain medications.

Cognitive-behavioral therapy (CBT) is a form of psychotherapy that is very effective in treating severe social anxiety. A major aim of CBT and behavioral therapy is to reduce anxiety by eliminating beliefs or behaviors that help to maintain the anxiety disorder. For example, avoidance of a feared object or situation prevents a person from learning that it is harmless.

A key element of CBT for anxiety is exposure, in which people confront the things they fear. The exposure process generally involves three stages. First, a person is introduced to the feared situation. The second step is to increase the risk for disapproval in that situation so a person can build confidence that he or she can handle rejection or criticism. The third step involves teaching a person techniques for coping with disapproval. In this stage, people are asked to imagine their worst fear and are encouraged to develop constructive responses to this fear and perceived disapproval.

These stages are often accompanied by anxiety management training—for example, teaching people techniques, such as deep breathing, to control their anxiety. If this is all done carefully and with support from a therapist, it may be possible to defuse the anxiety associated with feared situations.

If you undergo CBT or behavioral therapy, exposure will be carried out only when you are ready; it will be done gradually and only with your permission. You will work with the therapist to determine how much you can handle and at what pace you can proceed.

CBT and behavioral therapy have no adverse side effects other than the temporary discomfort of increased anxiety, but the therapist must be well-trained in the techniques of the treatment for it to work as desired. During treatment, the therapist will likely assign homework—specific problems that the patient will need to work on between sessions.

CBT or behavioral therapy generally lasts about 12 weeks. It may be conducted in a group, provided the people in the group have sufficiently similar problems. Supportive therapy, such as group, couples, or family therapy can be helpful to educate significant others about the disorder. Sometimes people with social anxiety also benefit from social skills training. Individuals suffering from social anxiety disorder should seek out a provider who is competent in cognitive and behavioral therapies.

Medications

Proper and effective medications may also play a role in treatment, along with psychotherapy. Medications include antidepressants such as selective serotonin reuptake inhibitors (SSRIs) and monoamine oxidase inhibitors (MAOIs), as well as drugs known as high-potency benzodiazepines. Some people with a form of social anxiety that presents itself only when they have to perform in front of others have been helped by beta-blockers, which are more commonly used to control high-blood pressure.

It is important to understand that treatments for social anxiety disorder do not work instantly and that no one plan works well for all patients. Treatment must be tailored to the needs of each individual. A therapist and patient should work together to determine which treatment plan will be most effective and to assess whether the treatment plan seems to be on track. Adjustments to the plan are sometimes necessary since patients respond differently to treatment. Overall, the prospects for long-term recovery for most individuals who seek appropriate professional help are good.

OBSESSIVE-COMPULSIVE DISORDER

Obsessions are more than thoughts we keep coming back to. They are constant, overriding all other thoughts, they are often impulsive and are typically inappropriate, forbidden socially or simply disgusting. These obsessions create a high level of anxiety and are referred to as "ego-alien" and "ego-dystonic" because they are typically completely out of character for the person dealing with them. The person will not be able to control the thoughts and may leave with a high level of fear that the thoughts will translate into an actual loss of control with the thoughts or impulses being acted out. Many people who are suffering from OCD may have irrational fears of germs or body fluids, or they could suffer from constant doubts that they have forgotten or overlooked something. The obsession might also center on a desire for things to be placed in or done in a certain order. They can also involve a fear of losing control, or the constant battle against impulses that are violent or sexual in nature.

When people suffering with OCD are faced with these obsessions and thoughts, they engage in compulsions to help ease the anxiety. The compulsions are repetitive, comforting behaviors or mental processes. Compulsions can be obvious and clear behaviors; such as checking, repetitive hand washing, or some other behavior. They can also be mental acts that are less obvious such as praying, reciting or counting. Compulsive rituals can consume many hours a day for some people. The rituals can be complex, taking up several hours; or several hours can be consumed on the repetitive tasks.

Some people are more neat and tidier than others naturally but someone who suffers with obsessive compulsive disorder takes neatness to the next step, to an extreme degree. A sufferer will spend many hours tidying, cleaning, checking and re-checking that objects are in order etc. to the point of it interfering with their everyday lives.

An obsession is a recurring thought, idea or image that although not making a lot of sense will continue to intrude on your mind. An example may be the thought of leaving your door unlocked, you recognize this fear as irrational but you cannot get it out of your mind, hence you repeatedly check and re-check that the door is locked.

A compulsion is the ritual you perform to dismiss the anxiety which has been brought on by the obsession. An example would be washing your hands continuously to dismiss the fear of being unclean or contaminated. You fully realize this ritual to be unreasonable but feel compelled to carry it out to ward off the anxiety associated with the compulsion.

Obsessions can occur independently of compulsions, it is thought that around 25 percent of sufferers will only struggle with obsessions, so the fear is there but they do not feel compelled to carry out the ritual to free themselves of the anxiety.

The most common of compulsions would be the hand washing ritual. You would be continually concerned about avoiding any contamination so much so you avoid coming into contact with anything associated with dirt or germs, an example here would be shaking hands with someone or even touching a door handle. You could literally spend hours washing hands to reduce your anxiety about contamination. It is thought that women are more likely to be compulsive about cleanliness but men would outnumber women when it comes to checking and re-checking items, as in the example of repeatedly checking if a door is locked.

It is common for obsessive compulsive disorder to first set in with males when they are in their teens to early twenties, and for females when they are first entering adulthood. The course of the disease can vary; but people can expect that the symptoms will become worse during periods of great stress. Certain disorders are commonly co-morbid with OCD; including major depressive disorder and generalized anxiety disorders. Roughly twenty to thirty percent of those people undergoing clinical trial for obsessive compulsive disorders report that they have previously experienced tics and another one-third of people suffering from OCD also have Tourette's disorder. Among people with Tourette's disorder, up to fifty percent of them will develop some form of obsessive compulsive disorder.

Obsessive-compulsive disorder is more often than not accompanied by depression and in some cases can also develop into phobic avoidance, for example, a sufferer will completely avoid public restrooms.

Obsessive-compulsive behavior was at one time considered a rare disorder but recent studies have shown that four or five percent of the world's population may suffer to a degree with this disorder. It is important for anyone who has obsessive-compulsive disorder to realize it has nothing whatsoever to do with being crazy or having a form of madness. You recognize that what you are doing is irrational and you are very frustrated that you cannot control your thoughts and actions.

Studies have shown that about half of all obsessive-compulsive disorders actually begin in childhood with the majority of the remaining cases developing in early adult life, a fairly small number of cases will appear in later life.

Obsessive compulsive disorder is clearly a genetic disorder that shows a higher level of familial specificity than many other anxiety disorders. First-degree relatives who have Tourette's disorder have a greater chance of developing obsessive compulsive disorder. There are many mental disorders that can fall into the category of obsessive compulsive disorders such as trichotillomania (compulsive hair pulling), sexual behavior disorders, compulsive gambling and compulsive shoplifting. These other conditions are not as ritualistic as those commonly associated with obsessive compulsive disorder; however they do provide the same level of pleasure or gratification. Another disorder than can occur comorbidly with OCD is body dysmorphic disorder; with this disorder, the compulsive and obsessive behaviors will center very specifically around some feature of a person's appearance.

For some the thought of Obsessive Compulsive Disorder Symptoms may seem a little funny but for those suffering from the disease find the thoughts far from funny. It is reported that some 2.2 million people are diagnosed with this disorder every year. When you factor that some of these people have already suffered for a few years before seeking medical treatment their daily quality of life has suffered for some time with debilitating thoughts and crippling actions to their everyday routine. You may feel as though you are alone and that there is no one in the world that can help you, but I am here to tell you that there are thousands of people who have had OCD and beat it, including myself!

Obsessive Compulsive Disorder Symptoms - Elaboration On Various Symptoms Of OCD

Obsessive compulsive disorder (OCD) consists of two parts. If you want to understand the symptoms of obsessive compulsive disorder, you should have the full understanding of both parts. The first part of OCD contains obsession while, the second part consists of compulsions. Now, I will separately elaborate both of the parts.

1). Obsessions. Obsessions are ill thoughts of a person with particular characteristics. These thoughts are not normal thoughts rather they are unwanted, penetrating and appear again and again in one's mind. This is the part which relates to mind of a person and, no other person can see it. Only the sufferer knows about his obsessions while, others may know through his overt behavior or verbalizations. Whenever these thoughts strike one's mind, they produce anxiety such as, the thought that one's hands are dirty. Whenever, this thought will come into one's mind, person will start feeling that his hands are dirty, and should be washed.

2). Compulsions. Compulsions are the repetitive, fixed-pattern behaviors. A person feels drive to perform these behaviors. We have seen that when obsessions come into one's mind, they produce anxiety. Thinking that one's hands are dirty, one gets anxious and feels compel to wash his hands in order to reduce that anxiety. Obsessions strike mind repeatedly, producing mental anxiety. As a consequence, person performs particular behaviors repeatedly to get rid of anxiety.

Sometimes, people are over conscious about certain things. For example, there may be a person who is over conscious about his hygiene. He may wash his hands several times during a day. Psychologists diagnose obsessive compulsive disorder when these symptoms take the form of ritualistic behavior and, start interfering in daily functioning of the person. A person with obsessive compulsive disorder may get one or two hours late from office because he was busy in washing his hands.

There are different types of obsession such as, concern with germs, dreadful happenings (death, fire), perfectionism, religious concerns, lucky or unlucky numbers, sexual and aggression impulses and counting things. Compulsions may include excessive handwashing and bathing, checking (doors, locks, emergency brakes), touching, ordering/arranging things again and again, counting, cleaning households and miscellaneous rituals (writing, speaking, moving) etc. people may suffer from one or more symptoms of obsessive compulsive disorder simultaneously. Sufferers know that their thoughts are ill, and their behaviors are inappropriate. In some of the cases, children leave their schools, because their obsession regarding cleanliness compels to leave the classroom and go for handwashing.

Generally, sufferers think that their ritualistic behavior (compulsions) will prevent them from obsessions. These compulsions reduce their mental anxiety for a brief period of time, but they keep on experiencing obsessions. Repetitive behaviors are observable in young normal children. Sometimes, it becomes difficult to distinguish between normal repetitive behavior and pure compulsive behavior. Usually it can be diagnosed when they grow older and, this is the time when their compulsions become firm. There is some difference between onset of the disorder among males and females. Males develop this disorder at an average age of nine whereas; females develop at an average at of eleven years. Moreover, children are more affected by compulsion whether; adults experience obsessions and compulsions at an equal base. The reason behind this may be that children are less likely to verbalize their mental processes and thoughts. Whatever the case, one should be vigilant about symptoms of obsessive compulsive disorder because, once they become fixed, they are most difficult to eliminate.

Obsessive Compulsive Disorder Causes - Elaboration On Various Causes Of OCD

Understanding the precipitating factors or causes of obsessive compulsive disorder (OCD) is essential because this disorder is most difficult to manage once it strikes an individual. Sometimes, there are some causes of disorders that can be controlled before the onset of the disorder. It is equally important to understand the various causes of a disorder because; causes are not same for all the sufferers. Management may be different for the sufferer who has adopted disorder from his family whereas, different for the one who has developed the same disorder after facing stressful family circumstances.

Obsessive compulsive disorder occurs at an early age and sometimes it is not differentiated from normal ritualistic behavior of the children. The disorder becomes obdurate till the time it is diagnosed. For such kinds of disorders, it is preferable to locate the causes of disorder for the sake of prevention.

There are different precipitating factors of OCD, and I will discuss each of them, separately.

1). Biological/Physiological Causes. Firstly, in most of the cases of obsessive compulsive disorder, we can find biological basis of the disorder. Empirical data has shown that individuals with OCD have first degree relatives with the same disorder. The idea of the biological basis of the disorder is strengthened by the co-morbidity of Tourette's syndrome and OCD which shows that the neurological factors which cause Tourette's syndrome, are involved in OCD, as well. Brain pictures of individuals suffering from OCD demonstrate abnormality in structure of basal ganglia. This is the brain structure which is located under cerebral cortex. Sometimes, antibodies react with strep cells and produce inflammation in cells of basal ganglia. This reaction can produce obsessive compulsive symptoms in an individual.

According to researchers, worry circuit in the brain seems to be involved in causing obsessive compulsive disorder. Worry circuit is a set of neurons that produce signals of danger and warns an individual in anticipation of a threatening situation. It is hypothesized that this circuit consistently sends messages regarding threat and demands for urgent attention. This condition leads to obsession and compulsive behavior eventually. Serotonin is the neurotransmitter which is involved in obsessive compulsive behavior. Lower levels of serotonin in brain can produce obsessions and compulsions in an individual. This is all about biological or physiological causes of obsessive compulsive disorder.

2). Reinforcement. Negative reinforcement makes compulsive patterns stable. Individuals indulge in compulsive activities because these activities reduce their mental anxieties. Once, the individual know that carrying out some behavior will reduce his anxiety; he makes a habit to perform those behaviors. Psychologists from learning perspective strictly follow their views about the role of reinforcement in development of different disorders.

3) Social Causes. Element of prevention becomes significant when we talk about social causes. Some social factors have the potential to induce obsessions and compulsions in an individual. For example, child sexual abuse is the factor that can produce obsessive compulsive behavior in an individual. Such children remain preoccupied with feelings of incest and try to clean their selves through repetitive bathing and handwashing. Parental neglect during childhood can also cause OCD. Any traumatic event that has potential to induce higher levels of anxiety, can be rated among causes of obsessive compulsive disorder.

Obsessive Compulsive Disorder Treatments

Obsessive compulsive disorder (OCD) treatments include a wide variety. Sometimes, clinicians (psychologists or psychiatrists) are unable to treat obsessions fully. In such situations, clinician tries to manage disorder as much as possible. In most cases, obsessions exist but, the patient learns to manage his anxiety, and prevents himself from indulging in compulsive or ritualistic behaviors.

Treating OCD takes time because obsessions are embedded in the mind and one finds it difficult to distract his mind. These obsessions produce anxiety. To reduce this anxiety, an individual performs compulsive behavior. Difficulties exist at two levels during treatment. Firstly, difficulty appears when an individual becomes habitual to reduce anxiety through compulsions. Secondly, difficulty appears when a clinician stops an individual to perform compulsion after occurrence of obsession.

Treatments for obsessive compulsive disorder includes a variety of techniques and therapies.

1) Pharmacological Treatment. Empirical researches have shown that neurotransmitter serotonin is involved in obsessive compulsive disorder. Low levels of serotonin can produce obsessions and compulsions in an individual. If this is the case, psychiatrists recommend Serotonin Reuptake Inhibitors. These inhibitors include Prozac, Paxil and Zoloft etc.

2) Psychotherapies. Different types of psychotherapies can be used for treating OCD.

The first thing, which a clinician can do, is to psychoeducate the sufferer and his family about the disorder. Psychoeducation consists of developing the full understanding regarding any psychological issue. When a clinician will psychoeducate someone about OCD, he will develop the full understanding of causes, symptoms and various treatment modes of disorder.

Clinicians widely use relaxation therapy as a treatment for obsessive compulsive disorder. In this kind of therapy, clinician teaches an individual to calm down himself. Self-talk or self-instruction is the technique which can be most beneficial for an individual with obsessive compulsive disorder. During self-talk, an individual talks to himself in order to guide. This self-talk is also helpful in preventing an individual from performing compulsions.

Treatments for obsessive compulsive disorder include family therapy. There are certain reasons for giving family therapy. Sufferer of obsessive compulsive disorder is already victimized in social gatherings for his repetitive behavior, but sometimes, family does not support its member, as well. During family sessions, family members of the sufferer are instructed to provide him social support and to empathize with the sufferer.

Exposure Response Prevention (ERP) is one of the most popular psychotherapies. In this therapy, the sufferer is exposed to anxiety provoking condition such as, the sufferer is asked to touch the handle of the door but, after that he is not allowed to wash his hands. In this way, his anxiety diminishes automatically, and sufferer learns that compulsive behaviors are not essential to reduce anxiety.

Hypnotism can be used to reduce symptoms of obsessive compulsive disorder. Hypnotist tries to reduce particular ritualistic behaviors through instructions. Cognitive therapy can be used for altering the meaning or interpretations of obsessions and compulsions. Mostly sufferers consider their obsessions as threatening that can cause harm for them. The task of the clinician is to challenge these obsessions and replace them with accurate thoughts. So all these therapies are included in the treatments for obsessive compulsive disorder and, these therapies can benefit a sufferer a lot.

PANIC DISORDER

Anxiety is a normal reaction that we all have when we are confronted with a stressful situation in our lives, but a panic disorder is a much more serious condition that can strike suddenly without any warning or reason. People with this disorder will have a panic attack which is a response to fear, however the response is normally out of proportion for the given situation. A person with a disorder will develop a fear overtime that they will have another panic attack. This constant fear of having another attack can eventually affect the daily functions and the overall quality of one's life. If not treated, having a disorder can ultimately rule your life. Normally serious conditions that include alcoholism, drug abuse or depression can greatly increase the probability that a person will develop a panic disorder.

People that suffer from a panic disorder experience a panic attack that can last around 10 minutes and even longer for more severe cases of panic disorders. When a person has a panic disorder and they suffer a panic attack, they often feel an intense and overwhelming feeling of terror, with difficulty breathing. A panic attack can also cause a pounding feeling in the chest and a dizziness feeling accompanied by a feeling that they may faint. Other symptoms can include sweating, nausea, and trembling or uncontrollable shaking. A panic attack can cause hot flashes or chills and a feeling of numbness or tingling. A panic disorder can be very dangerous if the proper treatment isn't sought. Experiencing a panic attack while behind the wheel of an automobile is not only scary, but can be dangerous. During a panic attack, a person my feel that they are losing control and that can be dangerous if that happens while driving.

Having a panic disorder can rule your life and make you very fearful to step outside of your door. One of the worst problems for people that have this disorder is the constant fear of suffering future panic attacks. Having this fear is how a disorder can easily start to rule your life. The fear of future attacks can cause a person to change many things in his or her daily routine, including avoiding certain places, situations and even driving or the willingness to travel because of that fear of having another panic attack.

An individual experiencing a panic attack feels an undeniable wave of fear for no particular reason at all. The individual heart begins to beat rapidly, his chest hurt and it became increasingly more difficult to breathe; at which time the individual believes he is having a heart attack and will die if he does not receive proper intervention.

One patient defined his symptoms in this way: I am so afraid; every time I start to go out I get that awful feeling in the pit of my stomach, and I am terrified that another panic attack is coming or that some other unknown terrible thing is going to happen to me or someone in my family."

Panic attack generally last no more than a few minutes, but it can be the most distressing condition that a human being can experience. Individuals who experienced one attack will have others. Those who experience repeated attacks, or feels heightened anxiety about having another attack are considered to have developed panic disorder.

Panic disorders are a serious health problem in the United States. Recent studies concluded that about three million people will experience panic attacks at some time during their lives. The symptom is strikingly different from other types of anxiety. Panic attacks are very sudden and often unexpected, seemingly unprovoked, and are often disabling.

When a person has sudden overwhelming fear and anxiety they are having what we call a panic attack (PA). The heart will pound and they find it hard to breath. They can feel dizzy and feel like they are going to vomit. Sometimes they feel like they will dye. If (PA) are not treated they can escalate into other problems and panic disorder. Severe cases can cause a person to withdraw from everyday activity. With treatment you can take control of your life once again and eliminate or reduce the symptoms.

Cynthia's story

Cynthia first had a (PA) about six months ago. When she had this attack she was in her office getting ready for an important meeting. Without any advanced notice she felt a very intense feeling of fear. After this she was feeling sick and felt as if she would vomit. Cynthia's heart was pounding and she was finding it hard to breath, her body was also shaking uncontrollably. After several moments the the attack had passed and she was feeling better. Cynthia became deeply worried about this as nothing like this had ever happened to her before.

About two weeks later Cynthia had her second (PA). From then on her attacks started happening more and more often. Cynthia is never sure when her next (PA) will come or where she will be. Out of a deep fear of having an attack while in public, Cynthia has been going home after work and staying there. Cynthia has also developed places she avoids such as elevators. She is not afraid of elevators just of having a (PA) while on one.

A (PA) can come on at any time without warning. Most of the time there is not a reason for the (PA). Panic attacks can even occur when you're relaxing or sleeping. (PA) can happen just one time or they can be something that happens repeatedly. Most people who suffer from (PA) have them repeatedly. Many times (PA) that are recurring, are triggered by a specific situation. These triggers can be things like high places, public speaking or riding in a car. This can be especially true if the situation has caused a (PA) in the past. Most of the time the (PA) comes on when you feel like you are in danger or cannot escape. You can have one or two panic attacks in your life and besides that you live a normal life. Sometimes (PA) can happen in association with panic disorder and depression. Whatever you may think, this is treatable. Many techniques have been developed to help deal with the symptoms.

Some of the symptoms of the onset of a panic attack

Most (PA) occur when you are not at home. You can have (PA) virtually anyplace - driving, at a party, taking a shower, at the grocery store.

The symptoms of a (PA) come on quickly and with very little warning. Most (PA) will be at their worst about ten minutes into them and be over in about twenty or thirty minutes. It is very rare for a (PA) to last more than one hour. A complete full panic attack can combine some or all the symptoms listed below.

✓ Hyperventilation or being short of breath

✓ Pounding or racing heart

✓   Pain or discomfort in the chest

✓   Shaking and trembling

✓   Feeling like you are choking

✓   Feeling like you are not connected or detached from your surroundings

✓   Perspiration

✓   Feeling like you are going to vomit

✓   Feeling lightheaded or faint

✓   Tingling sensations in your limbs

✓   Hot and / or cold flashes

✓   Afraid you could dye or losing control

A panic attack can feel like a heart attack.

Symptoms of a (PA) tend to be physical and sometimes these can be so bad, that people think they are having a heart attack. It is not uncommon for people who have panic attacks to make trips to the doctor, because they think they are having a heart attack. It is very important to have any possible problems checked out, but do not overlook the possibility of a panic attack.

Lots of people will experience a panic attack without ever having another one or any complications. Do not worry if you have had only one or two (PA). Be aware that if panic attacks persist you are most likely developing panic disorder. Panic disorder is having several, repeated panic attacks. Panic attacks combined with constant anxiety and changes in your behavior are most likely panic disorder.

Some Symptoms Of Panic Disorder

✓ You have frequent, sudden and unexpected panic attacks that are not related to a specific situation.

✓ You worry a lot about having more panic attacks.

✓ You are changing your routine because of the panic attacks, such as avoiding place you had a panic attack in the past

One panic attack can last only a couple minutes, but this one panic attack can leave a lasting negative impression on a person. Panic attacks that happen over and over can take a huge emotional toll on a person. Just the memory of the fear and overwhelming terror can hurt your self-esteem and create harmful disturbances in your life. This can lead to the panic disorder symptoms listed below.

Anticipatory anxiety - You feel anxious and tense between panic attacks. This is caused by the fear that you will have another attack.

Phobic avoidance - You avoid certain places and situations. You do this because you fear the place or situation will cause another panic attack. If you start avoiding places most the time, phobic can turn into agoraphobia.

Panic Disorder Causes

One approach to understanding the cause of panic disorder is that the body's normal alarm system the mental and physical mechanisms that allows a person to react to a threat, tends to be triggered unnecessarily, when there is no real danger in the immediate environment. Most medical studies are unable to explain exactly why this happens.

However, several psychological studies have showed, the root cause of panic disorder may begin on the emotional level or the physical side, or it could be both. The feeling of heightened-anxiety always begins with a trigger that initiates the fight or flight response from the limbic system. For example, the first hint of apparent danger your brain chemistry, blood hormones, and cellular metabolism all goes into action.

When you have a chronic anxiety disorder over time your anxiety symptoms may be triggered by less and less serious events because the limbic system has been sensitized to react in a highly panicky manner.

For example, if as a child you were constantly yelled at; as an adult you may feel anxious whenever there is potential for confrontation with an authority figure; and you may go to extreme measures to avoid such confrontation, even in a situation as benign as refusing a simple request by a family member or anyone of authority figure. At this point your conscious mind has lost track of the connection between your current feeling and your past emotional experience. You now have no idea why you are feeling panicky about something of so little significant.

No one knows exactly what the panic disorder causes are although there is evidence to suggest that it is the result of a combination of the following influences.

Genetics:

The chances are 8 times greater to develop this disorder if a family member, such as a parent or grandparent, also had it. Also, if one identical twin has it there is a 40% chance that the other twin will also get it.

Environmental/Social Factors:

Some panic disorder causes center around major stresses in life or in a person's upbringing. These include overprotective parents, parents who were always anxious, child abuse or some childhood trauma or high stress levels in the home, to name a few.

Other panic disorder causes may be attributed to the use of illegal drugs (cocaine, marijuana), drinking a lot of alcohol or caffeinated beverages, using certain medications that treat heart problems or asthma or ending the treatment of certain ailments like anxiety and sleeping disorders.

Medical Conditions:

Panic attacks can also be caused by other existing medical problems such as hyperthyroidism, certain heart problems, epilepsy and other seizure disorders as well as asthma.

Biological Factors:

There are a few theories here, one of which is that your fight or run reaction is triggered for no reason although researchers don't know why. Another theory is that when an imbalance of oxygen and carbon dioxide occurs in your system, a signal is sent out that you are going to suffocate which results in a state of panic. A third theory suggests the symptoms of a panic attack are caused by an imbalance of serotonin which is a chemical messenger in the brain that helps regulate anxiety.

Mode Of Treatments

There are a wide variety of treatments available for panic disorders, including several effective psycho pharmacology interventions, and specific forms of psychotherapy. Psychotherapy for panic disorder is equally important as drug intervention. Several studies shows that the combination of medication and psychotherapy treatment for panic disorder is more effective than either intervention alone.

Cognitive Behavioral Therapy (CBT) is widely accepted as the superior form of psychotherapy. CBT is designed to help those with panic disorder identify and decrease the irrational thoughts and behaviors that reinforce panic symptoms.

Psycho dynamic psychotherapy is another form of intervention that is seldom mentioned as an appropriate treatment for panic disorder. In fact, many therapist strongly reject the idea of using psycho dynamic techniques as an intervention to reduce the symptoms associated with panic disorder.

What set psycho dynamic therapists apart from the rest is their ability to recognize one indisputable fact: Panic states may, symptomatically, appear to be identical weather they are produce from a neurotic condition or from a manic-depressive state.

Clinical research indicated that neurotic type of panic states should be treated solely with psychotherapy; and manic-depressive states are to be treated with one

271

of the many effective anti-depressive drugs. Proper differential diagnosis is the super-highway to symptom reduction for all psychological disorders, including panic disorder.

Treating Panic Disorder With Psycho Dynamic Techniques

Although studies have shown the effectiveness of cognitive-behavioral and psycho pharmacological treatments; many patients fail to respond positively to these interventions or have had persistence or recurrence of symptoms. Given the high costs and reappearance of panic disorder; there is a need to explore treatment options.

Psychoanalytic techniques are commonly used to treat panic disorder but have rarely been exposed to the rigor of scientific research procedures. Such a study would highlight and describe the psychoanalytic concepts involved in understanding panic disorder. While at the same time proposes a more "client-friendly" psycho dynamic psychotherapy for panic disorder called panic-focused psycho dynamic psychotherapy.

The potential benefit of this form of therapy is based on the belief that panic patients have a psychological vulnerability to panic disorder associated with personality disturbances, relationship problems, difficulties tolerating and defining inner emotional experiences, and unconscious conflicts about separation, anger and sexuality. Psycho dynamic psychotherapy focuses more, but not exclusively, on these impairments than other therapies, including psycho pharmacology, potentially reducing vulnerability to symptoms recurrence.

Unconscious emotions

According to psychoanalytic theory, panic symptoms are based at least in part on unconscious fantasies and affect In fact, both clinical and research observation suggests that panic patients have special difficulties with anger feelings and fantasies, such as wishes for revenge. These wishes often represent a threat to important love ones, especially those we have a close attachment to; therefore triggering a panic attack.

Patients are often unaware of the power of these affects and the revengeful fantasies that accompany them. Becoming aware, by bring them to consciousness, of this negative aspect of mental life and render them less threatening are important components of psycho dynamic psychotherapy.

Panic Disorder With Agoraphobia!

Panic disorder is at its most severe when it becomes panic disorder with agoraphobia. Panic disorder with agoraphobia creates such anxiety that a person will do anything to avoid being in what he or she considers 'unprotected space'. Public places are feared as 'unprotected' merely because a panic attack could happen there.

When a panic attack sufferer begins to avoid public places, agoraphobia has set in. The agoraphobic tries to stop attacks by making his or her world very small.

Agoraphobics have difficult networks of fears that totally control their lives. Major symptoms of agoraphobia are:

✓   Frequent intense panic attacks and severe anxiety.

✓   Avoiding attacks by staying home all the time.

✓   Depending too heavily on others.

✓   Never wanting to be alone.

✓   Avoiding any place where you can't escape.

✓   Fear you'll lose control in a public place.

✓   Feelings of detachment plus isolation.

✓   Helpless feelings.

✓   A persistent feeling of unreality.

✓ A feeling that your body is not quite real.

✓ Twitching, trembling, or emotional outbursts.

Agoraphobics have symptoms which are periodically disrupted by panic attacks. Agoraphobics have very intense panic attacks. Heart attacks and agoraphobic panic attacks look and feel very similar. The following symptoms are typical during a panic attack:

✓ Trouble breathing.

✓ Extreme disorientation or dizziness.

✓ Feeling like you may faint

✓ Numbness plus tingling sensations.

✓ Blushing uncontrollably.

✓ Chest pain.

✓ Worry that you are dying.

✓ Thinking you are going crazy.

✓ Rapid pulse.

✓ A spike in blood pressure.

A disorder with agoraphobia is serious and will not got away on its own. Agoraphobia usually develops after years of panic issues.

The negative effects of panic disorder with agoraphobia come with social isolation, unemployment, and broken private relations. Panic disorder with agoraphobia can be successfully treated even though the symptoms are severe.

Early diagnosis is critical. Early treatment creates the fastest cure. Cognitive Behavioral Therapy (CBT) combined with systematic desensitization is the standard treatment for agoraphobia. Medication may also be prescribed.

CBT is a method for changing the way an agoraphobic thinks about fear and the world. Systematic desensitization actually desensitizes agoraphobics to fear so they never become afraid of specific stimuli.

Agoraphobics could start out by being asked to simply imagine leaving the house. When that can be done without panic, the next step might be to imagine opening the door. Stepping outside might be the final step. Agoraphobics are all different, but generally the prognosis for a full recovery is excellent.

Antidepressant medications may be prescribed to relieve the most intense symptoms. Drugs can improve the effectiveness of therapy. Agoraphobics may be weaned off medication when therapy is complete. Patients occasionally continue to take medications in order to maintain a full recovery.

Treating the panic problem early can prevent agoraphobia. The cause of panic disorder with agoraphobia is unknown. No other mental disorder is more common than anxiety and panic. Anxiety disorders are responsible for thirty percent of all the cash spent on mental illnesses.

Since panic disorder remains a major health problem in the United States it is important to continue to develop effective approach to its treatment. Panic-focused psycho dynamic psychotherapy will be a useful alternative or adjunct to cognitive-behavioral approach and medication. Psycho dynamic therapy addresses intra-psychic conflicts, defense mechanisms, and developmental issues not likely to be focused on in other therapeutic methods

Psycho dynamic approach also affect psychological factors that lead to vulnerability to recurrence panic state, or other difficulties connected with a panic disorder. A complete and randomized controlled trial should shed further light on the effectiveness of panic -focused psycho dynamic psychotherapy.

POST TRAUMATIC STRESS DISORDER

One of the most difficult forms of anxiety disorder to deal with is post-traumatic stress disorder, first recognized as shell shock and battle fatigue. These names themselves indicate a lack of understanding of what was happening with these soldiers, many of whom were accused of "faking" symptoms to avoid being sent back to active duty. In those early days it was quite disconcerting to watch pictures of soldiers "reliving" their traumatic experiences as though they were still happening. While it now is diagnosed as "post-traumatic stress", it is that same debilitating disorder that literally ruined the lives of so many military personnel. However, today, lives do not have to be ruined by this anxiety-related disorder if the situation is dealt with immediately and if treatment focuses on the root cause rather than individual symptoms. We will briefly look at some causes and effects, symptoms, and treatments of post-traumatic stress.

Post-traumatic stress disorder (PTSD) can be experienced by individuals either witnessing or actually experiencing some traumatic catastrophe. Such calamities might be: war, death of a parent or other loved one, major disaster (fatal accident, tornado, school attacks or killings), rape, child abuse, or any form of abuse against humanity. Quite understandably, post-traumatic stress disorder produces other results such as: extreme fear, anxiety, guilt, feelings of loss of control, anger, depression, which can lead to nightmares, amnesia, and even personality changes, to name just a few. With children, some after effects can be learning disabilities, self-abuse and attention difficulties.

Research reveals two specific symptoms of post-traumatic stress labeled arousal and avoidance symptoms. The arousal symptoms are moodiness, lack of concentration and memory, over-reactions and proneness toward violence while the avoidance symptoms are unwillingness or inability to remember the trauma, and reluctance to feel or talk about emotions. When discussing symptoms, it is important to understand that although sometimes symptoms may occur within two or three months, in some cases, it may be years before symptoms develop. And not every victim of these circumstances develops post-traumatic stress disorder; for many the symptoms may stop after a month or so. In such instances, the web is a source for programs dealing with these anxiety related symptoms, that may possible prevent the onset of PTSD.

Post traumatic-stress disorder can present itself in anyone who has suffered severe trauma. This trauma can be anything that produces intense fear or terror which could include assaults, rape, violent crimes against yourself or close family members and would include natural disasters such as earthquakes, severe flooding, plane crashes etc. The symptoms appear to be more severe and last longer if the trauma is personal as in the case of rape or other violent crimes.

Common Symptoms Are:

✓ Flashbacks - these feel so intense you feel you are reliving the trauma

✓ Nightmares - very common in post-traumatic stress disorder

✓ Loss of interest in activities you previously enjoyed

✓ Persistent anxiety

✓ Inability to sleep well - constantly waking up during the night

✓ Irritability - including outbursts of anger

✓ Feeling detached or estranged from others including family members

✓ Constant distressing thoughts of the traumatic event

✓ Avoiding activities which could possibly end in the traumatic event happening again

To be medically diagnosed as having post-traumatic stress disorders the symptoms must have been present for at least a month and be causing you extreme distress whilst interfering with everyday life to a large degree. Sufferers of this disorder tend to have symptoms of depression as well as chronic anxiety symptoms. If other people died as a result of the trauma then guilt is also a major symptom with the sufferer maybe having feelings of blame or responsibility for the event or simply feeling guilty that they have survived.

Post-traumatic stress disorder can occur at any age, in children the trauma will sometimes be re-enacted in their play or in upsetting dreams. In total this disorder is thought to affect around four percent of the population with a rise in the number of sufferers during wartime.

Treatment Methods Include:

Relaxation therapy - deep breathing and other relaxation methods

Exposure therapy - exposure to the situation will help you to realize it is no longer dangerous

Cognitive therapy - fearful thoughts are replaced with more realistic thinking

Support groups - helps the sufferer realize they are not alone

Medication - Here the most popular drugs being SSRI's, sometimes combined with the short term use of tranquilizers

One type of Post-Traumatic Stress Disorder develops when frequent abuse occurs in the home. This can have grave consequences for developing relationships in general and intimate relationships in particular.

It is a cliché that before you can be in a healthy love relationship you at first must be in love with yourself. This is a very true cliché. For someone to be loved they have to love themselves. But to love themselves they have to be first truly loved and cherished by their parents. Parents often feel love for their children, but it is much rarer to show the action of love in a consistent fashion. This means treating a child in a healthy, non-judgmental way. Often parents are too demanding in their expectations or have too many needs of their own, to be able to show that type of love. Even if they do, we live in such a perfectionist culture that children often do not feel that they measure up.

Whenever a child feels abandonment from one or both of their parents they internalize the hurt and the result is a feeling of not being good enough to be loved. This feeling is the feeling of shame. Even if parents are relatively healthy and loving a child can feel tremendous abandonment if their parents get divorced, if a parent is alcoholic, or if they simply work too much and not spend the amount of quality time a child needs. This often leads to a deep emotional belief that they are unlovable.

Later, they might realize on a conscious level that they are loveable and in turn desire real love. Consciously they look for healthy love, but subconsciously they search out those people who are incapable of showing real love. This is called a repetition compulsion. This problem becomes worse if the child has been physically, emotionally, or sexually abused.

They find true love boring and yearn for people to treat them poorly, which ratifies their feeling unlovable. They often become addicted to these abusive relationships and feel that they cannot live without them. They become intensity junkies instead of trying to experience true intimacy. Finding partners who cannot commit is another variation on this theme.

When a child is repeatedly abused in childhood, as is often the case in alcoholic families and families where a parent has sexually abused a child, Post-Traumatic Stress Disorder will likely develop in that child. PTSD is traumatic stress that overloads a persons' nervous system. This overwhelming stress creates shock in a person and dissociation between the three major brains and the body/brain. The dissociation also causes repressed energy that cannot be released fully so that the individual returns to balance or homeostasis.

This repressed energy and dissociation causes the symptoms of Post-Traumatic Stress Disorder. When a person cannot return to normal functioning they often develop a repetition compulsion in an attempt to resolve the problem.

A repetition compulsion is concept mastery gone awry. Concept mastery is one of the major ways in which human beings learn. If a person is trying to learn a task and does not quite complete it appropriately he or she will have a tendency to keep trying until they figure out the solution to the problem. This healthy tenacity helps us develop and grow as individuals and as a species.

This healthy tenacity however can at times turn into an obsession. This is what occurs in a repetition compulsion. A person will try to solve the problem in the same fashion over and over again without making any changes to their strategy in the fruitless attempt to master the situation. They often become desperate in their attempt to complete the action and solve the problem. They fail to realize that something is wrong with their approach. There is often a blind spot where the solution resides. Instead of looking at the problem in a different fashion and discovering a new way to respond, the person attempts the same technique over and over again which results in repeated failure and frustration.

This psychological dilemma is best illustrated by a sad, but all too common tendency. When a child has been sexually abused by a parent the child will dissociate, which essentially creates a hypnotic experience. The child will remember on some level and in great detail everything that has occurred. He or she will remember how they felt like a victim. They will remember what they were dressed in, the time of day, and the furniture in the room. They will also remember what the abuser was wearing, what tone of voice was used, and a number of other details.

The child will then have essentially two models of behavior. One will be a victim, and the other will be an abuser. This will be especially confusing because the abuser might well be seen as quite loving in other situations. The child will then want to find a black or white answer to their confusion. This concrete and absolute thinking is characteristic of a child's thinking under the age of twelve.

The way a child attempts to resolve this conflict is to internalize the two models. Essentially a civil war develops when one part of the child feels like a good person who has been victimized and the other part acts like the original abuser and tells the child that they are worthless. The problem has no resolution however, because the two sides are usually equally matched.

It sets up a hot spot where increased psychic energy resides. It also sets up a double goal. The child will feel they are loveable and want love, but also feel unlovable and want to be rejected. This conflict will be mostly subconscious. Consciously they will move towards success and love, but usually because of their blind spot they will either act in a way or connect with a person who fulfills their subconscious desire or rather conviction that they are unworthy and either fail or get rejected.

In the failed attempt out of this stalemate they often subconsciously recruit a third person. Although, an abused child will identify with both the abuser and the victim, they usually specialize and follow one model more than the other. Therefore, a person who identifies more with the victim is drawn towards an abuser as if by radar and an abuser is drawn towards the victim in like manner. Often, even if aware of their blind spot and consciously trying not to repeat they are invariably drawn into the same snare or repetition compulsion.

NET(TM) or Neuro Emotional Technique(TM) theory postulates that we create our own reality and that we are responsible for our own story. This means that even if the story of past abuse when a person is a child is accurate and valid we are still responsible for repeating it if we do not deactivate the repetition compulsion and neutralize the energy that is stuck.

This is why NET(TM) Neuro Emotional Technique? is so effective for the problem of Post-Traumatic Stress Disorder and repetition compulsions. PTSD is about delayed grief or to say it another way energy that becomes stuck. A large part of this traumatic energy gets stuck in the body and NET(TM) is incredibly effective in relieving this energy. It seems to have the effect of allowing the client to reestablish homeostasis and therefore drain the energy and original belief behind the repetition compulsion.

When used in tandem with insight oriented therapy to understand the reason behind the self-destructive behavior, and EMDR to assist in shifting the short term memory loop of the trauma to long term memory, NET(TM) seems to complete homeostasis by bringing the body back into balance. This has been a major breakthrough in the treatment for Post-Traumatic Stress Disorder.

SPECIFIC PHOBIA

I'm afraid of heights and small places. I can't stand in an elevator with too many people, or go shopping during a sale because I start to breathe heavy and feel there is no way out. I can't look down when I'm on a bridge, and I close my eyes when I'm with someone who is driving through a tunnel. After all, what happens if the bridge springs a leak and the tunnel floods?

Sound familiar?

Phobias are the unrelenting fears of a situation, activity or thing that causes one to want to avoid it.

It's common for us to have phobias or fears. How about a fear of heights (acrophobia) and a fear of closed in spaces (claustrophobia)? Come to think of it, what about a fear of flying over water? I have a friend who believes that drowning would be worse than crashing on land. Both would be horrific, but somehow she fears drowning more

What is a phobia? There are a lot of anxiety conditions out there that people have to deal with daily. Some are common and things we´ve heard of like agoraphobia and social phobia and some are less common or less well known. These conditions arise when the preoccupation with worry has become so acute that you are no longer engaging in your normal routines.

Some of the common fears that can turn into angst driven nightmares are normal things that many people get nervous over but don´t avoid entirely. For example, many phobias center on the fear of going to the dentist, fear of thunder or lightning, fear of illness or fear of animals or elevators. Some of these fears don´t have a daily impact on our lives but they can have long term effects on our health or mental wellbeing.

A phobia is simply an irrational fear that is intense and persistent. The fear is directed at a particular activity, situation or person. People with these problems will go to almost any length to avoid that which they fear. If you are worried about going to the dentist, decades may pass without a visit, you may ignore tooth pain, and try ways to self-medicate or simply ignore the discomfort and hope it goes away.

This approach could of course leave you with a serious medical problem. These conditions make you avoid activities and people even if you know you should not.

More than 10% of the American population suffers from excessive fear at one time or another. Phobias also affect more women than men. Most specific disorders like fear of animals, fear of the elevator and fear of airplanes can usually be explained by some triggering or traumatic event that happened in your formative fears.

A close encounter with a dog, a dog bite or threat might lead to a lifetime fear or anxiousness around dogs. The triggering event doesn´t have to be that obvious though, it could be you were scared by a TV program and had bad dreams about that topic for a few nights and developed an intense fear.

Both specific phobias and more pervasive problems like social phobia and agoraphobia can be dealt with. You can stop avoiding the things that frighten you and tackle new experiences in your life. Don´t let worry control your life any longer. Go see your daughter´s play, talk to your boss about a raise, and ask out the cute receptionist you´ve been in love with for years.

If you have a phobia, you know it. It can be anything and everything and it most likely comes with a name. There are three types of phobias, social phobias, which are the fears of public speaking, meeting new people and other social situations; agoraphobia, which is a fear of being outside; and specific phobias, like a fear of a particular item or situation.

Did you know that a fear of clowns is called "coulrophobia" or that a fear of needles is called "aichmophobia"?

As experts put it, you can actually be afraid of something but it doesn't become a phobia unless it interferes with your life or sense of well-being. If you are a business person and you are up for a promotion that involves lots of air travel and you already had a fear of flying, guess what, now you officially have a phobia.

I have a friend who went on a trip to the Holy Land in Israel and it took her a long time to make the down payment and go. Why? Not because she lacked the money, but rather, because she knew she would have to confront her fears. First, she couldn't get there without flying over water, and second, the large majority of the places she was going to visit were underground in caves and grottos. So, how did she do it?

Well, let's be honest. Because flying over water freaked her out so much, she had to take a sleeping pill. But, it wasn't long and she arrived safely and soundly.

Being only the start of her fears, she had an even harder time getting over the fear of small places, but she took it one situation at a time with baby steps. That's where she went right. It was the first location of her trip that she kind of just stood on the edge and scoped out the room below. As the tour went a long, she slowly inched her way closer. The fear was still there, but not as monumental as she confronted it slowly.

She found it hard, especially when she was celebrating mass in the place where the Catholics believe Jesus is buried. It was small, the wall space narrow, and there was a large group of people pushing and shoving to get a spot. And, even though she didn't think she could do it, she also understood that she couldn't 'NOT' do it. She told herself that she couldn't let her fear win and went for it. The people in her group understood and she rotated in and out as best as she could. She would take a lot of deep breaths and kept telling herself she could do it. Even though she couldn't stay in there for long, just long enough to see what she was there for, she was still able to face her fears.

It's hard to face fears we have. For my friend, she weighed out the pros and cons and took the steps she was able to, in order to get past those fears. This is one approach to facing your fears, but experts also say you should research your believed outcome in an attempt to lessen the fear as well. For example, an individual who is determined their plane will crash, may want to consider the statistics surrounding that.

The fight or flight response is our body´s natural way of protecting itself from the dangers of this world. If a wild grizzly bear is chasing you, you run. Your body does it automatically. If your child is drowning, you jump in after them. You don´t think about it, your body just goes into action.

Your body determines whether it´s best to fight or react or run. For people who have this adrenaline surge triggered, it is normally in response to appropriate situations. For phobia sufferers, this response kicks into action inappropriately, triggering panic attacks. The anxiety episodes are so upsetting, that many people strive, regardless of the consequences, to avoid a repeat performance.

This is what keeps phobic´s from engaging in life; the fear. The extreme, unchecked and inappropriate response of their bodies is upsetting and humiliating and very few people want to knowingly expose themselves to an increased chance of a panic attack. Therefore, caution, no matter how silly or intrusive, is usually the most common path taken when confronting this problem.

Symptoms

A specific phobia involves an intense, persistent fear of a specific object or situation that's out of proportion to the actual risk. There are many types of phobias, and it's not unusual to experience a specific phobia about more than one object or situation. Specific phobias can also occur along with other types of anxiety disorders.

Common categories of specific phobias are a fear of:

✓ Situations, such as airplanes, enclosed spaces or going to school

✓ Nature, such as thunderstorms or heights

✓ Animals or insects, such as dogs or spiders

✓ Blood, injection or injury, such as needles, accidents or medical procedures

✓ Others, such as choking, vomiting, loud noises or clowns

Each specific phobia is referred to by its own term. Examples of more common terms include acrophobia for the fear of heights and claustrophobia for the fear of confined spaces.

No matter what specific phobia you have, it's likely to produce these types of reactions:

An immediate feeling of intense fear, anxiety and panic when exposed to or even thinking about the source of your fear.

Awareness that your fears are unreasonable or exaggerated but feeling powerless to control them.

Worsening anxiety as the situation or object gets closer to you in time or physical proximity.

Doing everything possible to avoid the object or situation or enduring it with intense anxiety or fear.

Difficulty functioning normally because of your fear.

Physical reactions and sensations, including sweating, rapid heartbeat, tight chest or difficulty breathing.

Feeling nauseated, dizzy or fainting around blood or injuries.

In children, possibly tantrums, clinging, crying, or refusing to leave a parent's side or approach their fear.

Causes Of Specific Phobias

Before looking at the treatment of specific phobias, it helps to understand the causes because they can help guide the treatment. Specific phobias usually develop during childhood but can begin later in life.

Negative Experiences

Many phobias develop as a result of a negative experience, such as being attacked by an animal or trapped in a small space.

Phobias can also begin after you have heard about a negative experience. For example, hearing about a plane crash, without receiving the necessary reassurance, can lead to a specific phobia.

Family Environment

Fears can be learned. If one of your parents was overly afraid of an object or situation, you may also have learned to be afraid of something similar.

You learn fears not just from what parents say, but from what they show. Suppose you were startled by a spider as a child. If you ran to one of your parents, and they rushed you away from the spider, you learned that it's normal to be afraid of spiders. The next time you saw a spider you might feel anxious. If your parent continued to be overprotective, you might gradually develop and irrational fear of spiders. Your fear would not be based on facts, but on your parent's emotional response. It would be based on what they show not on what they say.

Substance Use

Adulthood phobias can be caused by substance abuse. Tobacco, caffeine, drugs, and alcohol can all increase anxiety and the risk of developing an anxiety disorder

Medical Causes

A number of medical conditions can cause anxiety symptoms. These include an overactive thyroid, hypoglycemia, mitral valve prolapse, anemia, asthma, COPD, inflammatory bowel disease, Parkinson's disease, and dementia among others. Your physician may perform certain tests to rule out these conditions. But it is important to remember that anxiety is more often due to poor coping skills or substance abuse than any medical condition.

Risk factors

These factors may increase your risk of specific phobias:

Your age. Specific phobias can first appear in childhood, usually by age 10, but can occur later in life.

Your relatives. If someone in your family has a specific phobia or anxiety, you're more likely to develop it, too. This could be an inherited tendency, or children may learn specific phobias by observing a family member's phobic reaction to an object or a situation.

Your temperament. Your risk may increase if you're more sensitive, more inhibited or more negative than the norm.

A negative experience. Experiencing a frightening traumatic event, such as being trapped in an elevator or attacked by an animal, may trigger the development of a specific phobia.

Learning about negative experiences. Hearing about negative information or experiences, such as plane crashes, can lead to the development of a specific phobia.

Complications

Although specific phobias may seem silly to others, they can be devastating to the people who have them, causing problems that affect many aspects of life.

Social isolation. Avoiding places and things you fear can cause academic, professional and relationship problems. Children with these disorders are at risk of academic problems and loneliness, and they may have trouble with social skills if their behaviors significantly differ from their peers.

Mood disorders. Many people with specific phobias have depression as well as other anxiety disorders.

Substance abuse. The stress of living with a severe specific phobia may lead to abuse of drugs or alcohol.

Suicide. Some individuals with specific phobias may be at risk of suicide.

How To Overcome Phobias

Perhaps the most tragic part of phobia and fear is that they prevent you from living life to the fullest. You may not want to go to certain places or experience certain events for fear it may trigger your phobia or fear. Regardless, phobia and fear prevent us from living a joyful, vibrant life.

Imagine what your life will be like when you are free. When you can be confident and at ease in situations where you used to feel phobic or fearful. Imagine what it will be like when you can talk about your former symptoms as though you are describing a movie where the character is someone else, not you. It is like you have a distant memory of it.

Here is a list of phobia cures and Treatment Options:

Hypnotherapy

Hypnotherapy helps to reprogram your unconscious minds processes that may be generating your fear. When these processes resolved, people are then free of the symptoms of phobia and fear is minimized.

You can overcome fears and phobias on the list of all phobias using hypnosis. Hypnosis and other forms of modern personal development allow you to enter a state of trance and then deliver suggestions to reprogram, control or eliminate the phobia entirely. Imagine how nice it would be to go into a classroom for a test and not have an anxiety attack, or to be able to go camping in the woods. It works - it really does!

Hypnotherapy is safe and works fast and is becoming one of the most popular treatment options on this list of phobia cures.

Neuro-Linguistic Programming (NLP)

NLP is basically the study and practice of how we create our reality. From the NLP viewpoint, your fear is the result of your programs or "constructs" that you have created that are outmoded and not functioning as you would like them to. With NLP, these constructs are identified, exposed and re-programmed so that your phobia is made vulnerable and subsequently minimized and very often eliminated.

NLP interventions are quite rapid and effective.

Meridian and Energy Psychology

Meridian and Energy Psychology is emerging as an excellent therapy for fears and phobias because in studies it is shown to be rapid, safe, effective and long -lasting. Energy Psychology is based on a theory and practice that has been around for a couple of thousand years. Energy Psychology has the same foundation or roots as acupuncture, except in this case there are no needles used. You could call it emotional acupuncture - without the needles.

Recent scientific studies have shown Energy Psychology to be very effective. The two main fields of this meridian and energy psychology are EFT and TFT.

Energy Psychologies have been shown to enable you to quickly and easily change your behaviors as well as your thought patterns changing, often very quickly. What's more, you develop skills and techniques that are useful for a lifetime in all situations.

Cognitive Behaviour Therapy

Cognitive therapy or cognitive behavior therapy is a kind of psychotherapy used to treat depression, anxiety disorders, phobias, and other forms of mental disorder.

It involves recognizing unhelpful patterns of thinking and reacting, then modifying or replacing these with more realistic or helpful ones. Its application in treating schizophrenia along with medication and family therapy is recognized by the NICE guidelines within the British NH

Cognitive Behaviour Therapy (CBT) is based on the idea that how we think (cognition), how we feel (emotion), and how we act (behaviour) all interacts together. Specifically, our thoughts determine our feelings and our behaviour. Therefore negative thoughts can cause us distress and result in problems.

Conventional Medicine

Next on this list of phobia cures is conventional medicine. The physiological responses to phobias such as having a fast pulse, sweating, high blood pressure, and so on, can be controlled by the use of beta-blocking drugs.

The body beta receptors are tiny areas scattered all over the heart, the arteries, muscles and elsewhere at which adrenaline and related hormones act when you have your phobic reaction. When these hormones contact the receptors their effect is to speed up the heart and constrict blood vessels, so increasing the blood pressure; and to widen the airway tubes in the lungs. All this happens in moments of stress and need for action. The beta-blocker drugs have the same general chemical shape as the adrenaline molecule and so fit into the receptor sites in the same way, effectively blocking them so that adrenaline, although present, cannot act.

Either way, fear is something we all face in some form or fashion. How we deal with it is varies from person to person. But, in no shape or form should we ever let fear get in the way of our dreams and where we are going. As former US President Teddy Roosevelt said, "I believe that anyone can conquer a fear by doing the things he fears to do."

AGORAPHOBIA

Agoraphobia is a type of mental health problem where a person gets fear of open spaces because person think there is a chance of having terror to these open spaces.

Because of this fear the person usually avoids to go open and public places such as fair, market, train, bus, flight, shopping plaza, shops or sometimes in a queue. The person affected goes out to these places only with the escort who should be family members or friends. Some people get affected by this disorder so severely that they feel it's safe to stay in home rather than going outside.

The fear of open spaces can be extremely embarrassing, and limits the person's social and personal growth in terms of academics, career and economic sustainability.

As per one study done by the NIMH (National Institute of Mental Health) about 1.8 million adult people of USA which is approximately 0.8 percent of the total population of adult living with this mental disorder. The average age of the people with this mental disorder is 20 years.

Most people have heard of most phobias. Mention claustrophobia, social phobia, or arachnophobia and everyone pretty much knows what you are talking about. Mention agoraphobia, and most people will just shake their heads.

Because of this, many people who get agoraphobia often take a year, and in some cases, many years, just finding out what is wrong with them. Since the panic and anxiety symptoms that come with agoraphobia are so physical, people who get agoraphobia commonly visit a succession of doctors trying in search of a diagnosis. Since medical doctors are not usually trained to diagnose agoraphobia, let alone anxiety disorders, agoraphobia has had time to become deeply rooted in most people before they know enough about the disorder to seek the proper treatment and being recovery.

In light of this, here are some basics about agoraphobia:

Agoraphobia is "anxiety about, or avoidance of, places or situations from which escape might be difficult (or embarrassing) or in which help may not be available in the event of having a panic attack or panic-like symptoms." (DSM-IV)

Agoraphobia is a type of anxiety disorder. The term "agoraphobia" comes from the Greek words agora (αγορά), meaning "marketplace," and phobia (φόβος), meaning "fear." Literally translated as "fear of the marketplace," people with agoraphobia are afraid of open or public spaces.

In reality, most people with agoraphobia are not so much afraid of open and public places as they are afraid of having a panic attack in these settings, especially settings in which there may be no one to help in the case of a panic attack or actual emergency.

Symptoms Of Agoraphobia

The symptoms of the agoraphobia can be categorized into three areas viz. physical, behavioral and psychological. The physical symptoms can be observed easily when the people affected with it will find himself or herself in crowded open place. The physical symptoms may include:

- ✓ Uneven heart rate or Heart pounding

- ✓ Excessive sweat and hot

- ✓ Short of breath

- ✓ Fainting sensation

- ✓ Nausea and trembling in body

- ✓ Pressure in stomach

- ✓ Feeling of motion or bowel upset

- ✓ Darkness in front of eyes

- ✓ Chill or hot flush in the body

- ✓ Chest pain

    ✓   Numbness/tingling sensation in body (mainly in fingers and foot).

The behavioral symptoms may include:

    ✓   Unable to leave home - People affected try to avoid such environments which they feel that can trigger their anxiety and remain confined to home.

    ✓   Safety Concern - Sufferer are over concern about their safety and only go out after several spells of reassurance from somebody who is very close to the patient like family members or close friends. In some cases the patient demands for escort to go out in open environment.

    ✓   Escape - The patient affected usually tries to leave the anxiety triggering places or situations and straight back to home.

The psychological symptoms may include:

    ✓   Feelings of unreality

    ✓   Fear of crowds

    ✓   Feelings of choking

    ✓   Fear of dying

    ✓   Fear of losing control

✓   Social Isolation

✓   Fear of panic attacks

✓   Fear of staying alone

✓   Low self-esteem and self-confidence

✓   Dependency on others for most of the out of home activities

Remember that these one or more symptoms can vary from individual to individual case and it can also vary from the level of severity e.g it may be of mild level problem to severe level problem in different individual.

Causes Of Agoraphobia

The exact cause of agoraphobia is not known but experts give different hypothesis which are related to some or more with physical and psychological factors.

Overuse of medicines - Long term dependency on medicines which induced sleep and pain relief has been linked by the experts for the induction of agoraphobia. Drugs such as benzodiazepines (Alprazolam and Diazepam), tranquilizers (piperazine, phenothiazines, butyrophenes etc) and other sleeping medications have been linked to agoraphobia. These drugs are mostly prescribed as treatment of anti-psychotic syndromes.

Alcohol and tobacco dependency - Experts have also linked the overused of alcohol and tobacco in the development of agoraphobia. The direct dependence on chemical related to alcohol and tobacco overdose i.e ethyl alcohol and nicotine has a capacity to distort the brain chemistry and can further lead to agoraphobia. Some people take drugs with alcohol to enhance mood which has also potential to aggravate agoraphobia.

Spatial Orientation - Expert has related that the sufferers with agoraphobia have usually poor vestibular function which helps the body orientation with the spatial condition. Vestibular organ is a component in inner ear which helps the body in spatial condition such as deep inside the water or in dark place.

Frequent Panic Attack - Experts also suggested that agoraphobia is severe form of panic disorder in which sufferer gets regular intuition about attacks or freighting situations. Sometimes sufferer gets intuition and fear about dying without any apparent reason. Sometimes suffers may link any previous situations with their intuitions and try to justify their avoidance from escaping such situations.

Other Factors - It may be a disturbing childhood with history of abuse, accident, marital discord among parents, drug abuse, mental illness, depression syndrome or experience with any natural (cyclone, earthquake) or manmade calamities (such as war, chemical hazard, fire etc).

Diagnosis Of Agoraphobia

Usually there are no medical or laboratory tests to diagnose agoraphobia in the lab. Most of the experts use screening interviews to ascertain that the person is suffering from agoraphobia.

A general practitioner is the one who usually diagnoses the symptoms of agoraphobia, with the help of; Diagnostic and Statistical Manual of Mental Disorders (DSM-IV). This manual is published by the American Psychiatric Association and it is a guidebook used by entire mental health professionals to diagnose different mental conditions and it is also used by insurance companies for the reimbursement of treatment.

GP usually takes the help of psychiatrist who examines the sufferer history and symptoms through different detailed interview process. A psychiatrist is a medical professional who deals with problems of mental disorders.

The psychiatrist also strives to locate whether agoraphobia has any link with another mental health conditions. In such situations the identified mental health condition needs to be addressed as a priority before treating agoraphobia.

Manual of DSM-IV (American Diagnostic manual) and ICD-10 (European diagnostic manual) has led down the criteria for the diagnosis of agoraphobia. Both the manuals differ on presence of different criteria for diagnosis of agoraphobia but 'avoidance or escaping from the anxiety situation' is one of the diagnostic criteria which are common in both the manuals.

The manual of DSM-IV has described that a patient is suffering from agoraphobia:

 ✓ If the patient gets anxiety or get panic attack like symptoms in a open space

 ✓ If the patient avoids crowded places

 ✓ If the patient seek the help of family person, friend or cohort while going to open spaces.

 ✓ If the patient cannot able to provide any satisfactory explanations about his or her own behaviour.

ICD-10 has described that a patient is suffering from agoraphobia if any of these two criteria's are presented by patient:

✓ Anxiety in crowded place

✓ Fear in going out from home

✓ Anxiety in traveling alone or

✓ Fear in traveling out from home.

Treatment Of Agoraphobia

The clinical team usually prefers to go forward with the situation analysis of an individual. Some patients have only mild level of problem hence they need to go for only some sessions of psychotherapy but in other cases where the problem is severe the combination of psychotherapy and medication is used. In most of these severe cases patient receives the treatment well and they learn to keep phobia under their control.

When agoraphobia is associated with other panic disorder, treatment begins with creating a learning platform for the patient so that the patient understand the problem related to panic and patient can develop response slowly to overcome his or her panic. Usually small activities are planned in between the sessions to give the patient firsthand experience to overcome his or her anxiety disorder.

Later the problem tree of agoraphobia is constructed to design mode of treatment with the situation analysis of problems of the patient.

Medical Treatment

Antidepressants and anti-anxiety drugs are generally prescribed for agoraphobia. 'Imipramine' is one of the famous tricyclic category antidepressants and effectively used to treat agoraphobic symptoms. Venlafaxine is the another option for the experts which has proved effectively for long-term treatment of agoraphobia while TCA is considered as second option for the treatment of panic disorder when patient do not respond adequately to SSRI. SSRIs class antidepressants (sertaline or fluoxetine) which are actually selective serotonin reuptake inhibitors are also used for the treatment of agoraphobic situation. But these drugs have potential to gives side effects such as:

- ✓ Nausea and vomiting sensation

- ✓ Dizziness and headache

- ✓ Sleeplessness and restlessness

- ✓ Sexual dysfunction

Benzodiazepines such as alprazolam is also used for panic disorder treatment, but long duration usage of this medicine can create tolerance and dependency and overdose may have side effects such:

- ✓ Balance and orientation loss

✓   Loss of memory

✓   Lethargy and perplexity

✓   Fainting sensation

It is the medical experts who usually decide the doze and selection of the medicine and in some cases doctor tries out trial and error method before selecting the right shot for the patient. Doctor normally increases the doze of medicine to get the appropriate results and slowly reduces the doze at the end of treatment before finally stopping it.

Psychotherapeutic Treatment

Psychotherapeutic treatment is branch of psychology which uses the different psychotherapeutic techniques to deal with different mental disorders.

Cognitive-behavioural therapy (CBT) - It is the best experimented technique which is used for the treatment to agoraphobia. It has two components. First component focuses on exploration about agoraphobia and panic attacks and methods to control them and the other component focuses on coping mechanism of agoraphobia such as self control exercises. Through this therapy a patient learn about the symptoms of panic situations and their initiators as well as about the basic of relaxation therapy to control his or her anxiety.

For example, patient with agoraphobia have the thought that if he or she will use the train as a transport there will have an accident and eventually he or she will die in that accident.

The therapist usually start the therapy with desensitization exercise in which anxiety stimulus is provided to the patient in small and structured way so that the patient initiates a stimulus to overcome its anxiety. Slowly with each session the therapist increases the stimulus of anxiety so that the patient learns to response those stimuli with the help of therapist under guidance. Therapist usually chooses to initiate the session from patient home because the therapist office may have several initiators to increase the anxiety level. CBT usually consists of 10 -15 sessions, with each session length last for an hour.

Exposure Therapy (ET) - Experts usually combine Cognitive Behavioural Therapy (CBT) with exposure therapy. Exposure therapy can provide long term solution to most of the patients with agoraphobia and panic disorders. Departure of residual agoraphobic symptoms and not simply the occurrence of panic attacks is the sole aim of the exposure therapy. Systematic desensitization is also used with exposure therapy as it is known fact that patients can deal with exposure easily if a friend or close companion remain with them during the exposure therapy.

Therapist gives small exposure to the patient in initial session so that the patient reacts and develops control on its anxiety. e.g. by giving exposure on buying some grocery to nearby shop or paying electricity bill in nearby center and then gradually the exposure increases once the patient gets confidence and react perfectly on small exposures.

Relaxation Therapy (RT) - Relaxation techniques are also useful techniques to control for the agoraphobic as they make necessary endurance level in the patients to so that they can stop or prevent stimulus of anxiety. It is based on the thought that people affected with agoraphobia are very restless and their ability to relax themselves goes away with the anxiety. The relaxation therapy uses different methods to teach the patient to relax. It is easy therapy to learn and costs very less.

Different relaxation techniques are:

- ✓ Control and slow the breath rate

- ✓ Mediation

- ✓ Lowering of blood pressure through slowing heart rate

- ✓ Counting breath and number technique

- ✓ Control on anger and depression

✓ Increasing self-esteem and confidence to handle problems

The three steps guide for relaxation is:

1. Identify the sign of beginning the tension and fear

2. Start using relaxation technique to relieve tension and fear

3. Practice every day the same technique to prevent the feeling of tension and fear.

Alternative Medicines - Some alternative techniques are also used as a choice for treatment of acrophobia. These are:

Hypnotherapy - The expert hypnotherapist will hypnotize the mind and try to remove the negative thoughts by stimulating the positive thoughts.

Reiki- It is the ancient Japanese technique in which reiki expert use its hands to remove negative energy from the body and induce the positive energy in the body to make the patient healthy. This therapy works on energy transfer and sort of cleaning the body and mind

Complications of agoraphobia

Severe complications may arise if the symptoms of agoraphobia are not taken seriously. The physical and social mobility of the patient hampers in the initial stage and later the person have to live in isolation without any social contact.

The economic capacity of the person reduces as the job prospects are also hampered. The educational as well as other learned skills are eroded slowly and the patient is not able to compete anywhere in the market. It further leads into the vicious cycle of depression and severe anxiety. The person deteriorates his or her health and economic capacity and it further leads him or her to substance abuse like alcohol or drug abuse.

Simple lifestyle changes and self-help techniques to control anxiety

Controlling anxiety not only helps in controlling panic attacks and agoraphobia but it also helps in controlling other health problems like high blood pressure, depression and heart problem.

These self-help techniques are:

Walk slowly and start deep breathing. Be patient and concentrate to increase the deep breath as anxiety will make the situation worse.

Start Counting - Don't be panic with your anxiety but try to accept and reassure yourself. Start counting 1-10 and again back 10 -1 and try to divert from the trigger points.

Meditation- Meditation helps you to understand your strength and weakness. It also helps the person to concentrate strongly in case of anxiety.

Positive - Be positive. Don't fear from accepting the weakness. But take a challenge to face the situation with positive determination.

Change in lifestyle techniques which can also help:

Regular exercise like brisk walking, cycling or swimming relieves anxiety and enhances self-esteem.

A timely nutritional diet makes you active and prompt.

Reduce smoking as it will reduce nicotine from the body as well as the negative particles.

Reduce intake of alcohol and go for fruit juice and veggies.

Take proper sleep and rest to your body and mind

Become social with more interaction with family, kids and friends.

If possible enroll with some pet club or some charity club.

With the advancement of science and medicines no special treatment has been developed to fix agoraphobia problem. Experts are using various combinations of behavior, medicinal and cognitive therapies for getting the desired results and these combinations are showing the best results. The major difficulty in treating the agoraphobia disorder is lack of trained specialist in the field.

Lack of proven medicines is also one of the pitfalls in dealing agoraphobia. Most of the drugs are psychotic in nature and they deals with removing the symptoms temporarily and cannot treat the root causes of agoraphobia. Furthermore, medicines overdose and long usage can bring dependency as well as chances of severe side-effects. The best method is to use multiple therapies under the guidance of an expert for the greatest benefit.

DEPRESSION

Depression is a relatively common affliction. The lifetime prevalence for depression is about one in five. In other words, one in every five people will experience depression at some point in their lives. Of course, everyone experiences emotional low points in their lives, it's a normal part of being human. In people with depression however, this reached a point where quality of life is significantly impaired and, if left untreated, can have dire consequences, including loss of life, relationship problems and employment issues.

'People are not disturbed by events but by the view they hold about them.' Epictitus

This principle is at the heart of nearly all emotional and behavioural change. It can be challenging particularly if at the moment you are feeling depressed.

There are many different types of depression. Some forms are biological like clinical depression. Here the depression may not be a reaction to something that has happened but more of a chemical imbalance. This is best treated with medication and then with therapy. Other types of depression include 'reactive depression'. This type of depression is usually triggered when loss or failure is experienced and you end up feeling stuck in it.

The emotion of depression is commonly felt with other emotions like anxiety, anger, guilt but whereas anxiety is an emotion about something that might happen, depression is an emotion to something that has happened. So you may feel depressed about failing at something, losing something or someone. You may even feel depressed about the fact that you have been in state of stress or anxiety and now think this is how it will always be for me i.e. you believe that you have lost your old self or failed at solving your anxiety issues.

When you feel depressed, you feel like the sun has gone out of your life and more significantly that that it won't come back again. It's a state when you think that the future is all dark and bleak and you lose all sense of hope. You will also experience a number variety of physical symptoms. For example, you may feel very tired and lethargic and your appetite may be affected. You may just want to curl up and sleep the depression away.

Sadness is the healthy version of depression. Sadness is also triggered when loss or failure happens but it is an emotional state that you naturally heal from. When you feel sad, you feel like at the moment the sun has gone out your life but more significantly you retain your sense of hope for the future, unlike when you feel depressed. So what causes the feelings of depression and sadness? The quote above gives the answer. It is our view point, attitude or more simply the way that we think about what has happened that causes our feelings. Your beliefs about your loss or failure can cause depression or sadness. This is good to know because we can change our beliefs or thinking. It means that change is possible in the here and now. It shows that we can free ourselves from negative and unhelpful thinking patterns and behaviour. It shows that we are not slaves what happens to us even if the things that happened were very bad.

All of us have two types of thinking patterns or beliefs, beliefs that are healthy (rational) and beliefs that are unhealthy (irrational). Healthy beliefs lead to emotional well-being and enable you to achieve your goals and to move on and heal yourself when something bad happens. Beliefs that are unhealthy lead you to feel stuck and disturbed and cause you to do things that sabotage your healing.

Healthy beliefs are flexible and are based on the things that you want, the things that you like, the things that you desire and prefer but they are realistic and consistent with reality. This means they are accepting that sometimes you may not get what you want. Reality shows us that. An example of a healthy belief about loss may be 'I would have liked not to have lost my relationship but I accept that I did. This does not mean I am an unworthy or a Failure. I'm worthy but fallible. My worth does not depend on my loss'. Essentially, you do not put a condition on yourself despite your loss or despite your failures. This type of belief would cause sadness about the loss but not depression.

Symptoms Of Depression

The essential features of depression include depressed mood (feeling sad, hopeless, and empty) and loss of interest or pleasure in nearly all activities most of the day, nearly every day, for at least two weeks.

Depressed mood (or irritability for kids) and diminished pleasure are the primary symptoms people are cautioned to look for when depression is suspected.

While those symptoms certainly are red flags, the truth is that depression doesn't always look like debilitating sadness. Some symptoms of depression can be far more subtle. Those same symptoms can also mimic other medical conditions or be dismissed as normal everyday problems.

Identifying and understanding symptoms of depression are important first steps toward getting the proper supports in place to work through. Check out these less obvious symptoms of depression.

Physical pain

Complaints of physical pain are common in people with depression. Back pain, joint pain, and limb pain are all symptoms of depression and can result in chronic pain if left untreated.

Studies show that the link between pain and depression is a shared neurologic pathway, and that the worse the painful physical symptoms, the more severe the depression.

If you experience back pain, neck pain, or other sources of pain more often than not, don't be so quick to brush it off. It just might be a red flag of depression lurking beneath the surface.

Grouchy is your new normal

If it feels like even the slightest trigger sends you into a rage, or you feel irritable and grouchy a lot, you might be struggling with depression.

Although symptoms of hostility, anger, and irritability are not central to the diagnosis of depression, research shows that these symptoms are highly prevalent in depressed people and associated with increased depressive severity, longer duration, a more chronic and long-term course of depression, and high co-morbidity with substance abuse and anxiety.

You drink more alcohol than usual

One drink after a long day might take the edge off, but if you find that you're drinking a few drinks every night, it's probably more than a hard day at the office that's driving your behavior.

The interplay between heavy drinking and depression is complex. While some people might pick up a drink to cope with, or mask the feelings associated with, depression, heavy alcohol use can trigger a depressive episode. This is referred to as "substance-induced depression." One long-term study found that for men with alcohol problems, almost one-third of reported depressive episodes were only seen during bouts of heavy drinking.

Big changes in weight

Rapid weight loss or weight gain (a change of more than 5% of body weight in a month) is associated with depression. Depression can either zap your appetite to the point where you rarely feel hungry or cause you to overeat.

While it's perfectly normal to crave comfort foods when under stress, if you experience noticeable changes in your appetite that trigger weight loss or gain, you should seek an evaluation.

You forgot to shower

Depression can impact your daily living, including your self-care routine. If you find that you're not showering regularly, brushing your hair, practicing proper oral hygiene, wearing clean clothes, or struggling to even get out of bed in the morning, you might be in the midst of a depressive episode.

You can't make up your mind

Depression diminishes the ability to concentrate, including making decisions. whether you struggle to make a decision about your morning coffee or find that you're paralyzed when making important decisions at work, your depression slows your cognitive processes.

You feel really, really overwhelmed with guilt

Do you apologize for every little thing? Are you completely overwhelmed with feelings of guilt nearly every day? Excessive guilt is a sneaky sign of depression that might take you by surprise.

The sense of guilt associated with depression can include guilty preoccupations over perceived past or present failings. It can also include an exaggerated sense of personal responsibility for trivial matters and increased self-blame.

Causes Of Depression

Approximately 19 million Americans suffer from depression in a certain point of their lives. With this high incidence rate, it is necessary that we should all know the causes of depression so that proper precautions can be applied earlier to prevent it from developing. However, depression has no exact known cause, but there are risk factors that have been linked with the onset of depression.

Theories

Some theories state that chemical changes that occur in the brain are one of the most common causes of depression. These chemicals, which are known as the neurotransmitters, are responsible for carrying signals to and from the nerves and brain. When there is an imbalance in the production of these chemicals, depression occurs.

Family History

People with relatives who have been affected with depression have higher chances of developing the condition themselves. There is a possibility that depression can run in families for generations.

Stress and Trauma

Stress and trauma is one of the leading factors that can cause depression. This happens most especially to those people who have low emotional intelligence. Also, those who can't easily cope up with problems are at higher risks. Most common problems that can lead to stress and depression are breakup of a relationship, financial crisis, death of a loved one, and losing a job, just to mention some. Additionally, people who keep their problems to themselves are also at risk for depression compared to those who open up their problems to friends or family members.

Pessimistic Personality

People who always think negatively or always have a negative outlook in life are at higher risk for developing depression. Same goes to those people who have low self-esteem.

Psychological Disorders

Psychological disorders such as schizophrenia, eating disorders, substance abuse, and anxiety often appear together with depression. This is because these disorders are also caused by chemical imbalances in the brain.

Physical Conditions

There are some medical conditions that are known to contribute to depression, such as cancer, HIV, and heart disease. This is mainly because these conditions can cause stress and physical weakness to the affected person. In some cases, medications that are used to treat physical conditions can cause depression. This goes true to those medications that act directly on the chemicals of the brain.

So far, these are the known risk factors and causes of depression. It is vital that if you are suffering from this kind of mental disorder, that you seek treatment at once. This condition is a very serious illness but can be treated with proper and early treatment. When choosing the treatment, choose those that are 100% safe, fast acting, and that can cure the condition permanently, such as the natural remedies for depression. These natural remedies are safe and don't have side effects since they are made from natural ingredients.

Cbt Therapy For Depression

Cognitive Behavioral Therapy (CBT) is a abbreviated form of psychological used in the direction of adults and children with natural depression. Its focusing is on prevalent issues and symptoms versus more traditional forms of therapy which tend to focus on a someone's past yesteryear. The usual format is weekly therapy sessions coupled with daily praxis exercises designed to help the sufferer apply CBT skills in their home surroundings.

CBT for depression involves respective important features: identifying and correcting unfaithful thoughts associated with depressed sensitivity (cognitive restructuring), helping patients to pursue more often in gratifying activities (behavioural activation), and enhancing problem-solving skills. The first of these components, cognitive restructuring, involves cooperation between the patient and the expert to reckon and modify habitual errors in thinking that are associated with depression. Depressed patients often undergo contorted thoughts about themselves (e.g. I am stupid), their environment (e.g. My life is direful) and their prospective (e.g. There is no sensation in going forward, nothing will work out for me). Message from the patient's current experience, bygone history, and future prospects is used to counter these distorted thoughts. In addition to self-critical thoughts, patients with depression typically cut back on activities that have the possible to be enjoyable to them, because they expect that such activities will not be worth their exertion. Regrettably this usually results in a deplorable cycle, wherein dispirited mood leads to less activity, which in turn results in further depressed mood, etc.

The second portion of CBT Therapy, behavioral activation, seeks to remediation this downward spiral by negotiating increases in potentially satisfying activities with the patient. When patients are depressed, problems in daily realistic often seem insurmountable. In the final, the CBT therapist provides and counsel in special strategies for solving problems (e.g. breaking problems down into small steps).

Cognitive Behavioral Therapy is a scientifically well-established and effective treatment for depression. Over 75% of patients show noteworthy improvements.

EXPOSURE THERAPY

Exposure-based techniques are some of the most commonly used CBT methods used in treating anxiety disorders. One theoretical framework for understanding the rationale for exposure-based treatment comes from emotional processing theory. According to emotional processing theory, fear is represented by associative networks (cognitive fear structures) that maintain information about the feared stimulus, fear responses (e.g., escape, avoidance, psychophysiological responses), and the meaning of the stimuli and responses (e.g., tiger = danger, increased heart rate = heart attack). When a stimulus in the environment is encountered that resembles the feared stimulus, these associative networks activate the fear structure. The fear structure is pathological when the relationship among stimuli, responses, and their meaning do not match reality, such as when it is activated for safe stimuli or responses that resemble the feared ones. Furthermore, the fear structure is maintained by avoidance behaviors which do not allow for new learning to occur.

Exposure is proposed to modify the pathological fear structure by first activating it and then providing new information that disconfirms the pathological, unrealistic associations in the structures (e.g., tachycardia does not lead to heart attack, crowded malls do not lead to violent attack). By confronting the feared stimulus or responses and integrating corrective information in the fear memory, fear is expected to decrease. Exposure can take several forms including imaginal, in vivo (in real life), and interoceptive. Imaginal exposure occurs when the patient vividly imagines the feared situation/consequences and does not avoid their subsequent anxiety. In vivo exposure involves gradual approach to places, objects, people, or situations that were previously avoided although they are safe. Interoceptive exposure, which is mostly used in treating panic disorder, involves deliberately inducing the physical sensations the patient fears are indicative of a panic attack. These exposure techniques are similar in their function because they allow the patient to acquire new learning in order to modify the fear structure. In general, exposure therapy is of limited duration and is typically completed in about 10 sessions.

The difficulty many people have in choosing exposure therapy is that they feel as if they are going to be forced to face whatever situation or thing that is currently troubling them. If something makes you extremely uncomfortable, it would seem like an obvious choice to avoid it. However, delaying the inevitable will only serve to worsen the condition. However, what most people don't realize is that this type of therapy involves gradually working up to the things and situations that cause you discomfort and, all the while, encouraging you to relax throughout the entire process.

The most basic explanation of exposure therapy is a systematic desensitization to that which causes you anxiety. For example, if you fear insects, you would not start out with being exposed to one directly. Instead, the therapist would assess your particular threshold and start out at a level that does not make you anxious. Perhaps viewing a picture of an insect is too much for you to handle in the beginning, but talking about them does not make you uncomfortable. In this case, the therapist would most likely start out by discussing insects while teaching you relaxation techniques.

Let's look at an example of exposure therapy.

Let's say that you suffer from panic attacks and just the thought of going to the mall makes you incredibly anxious.

What the therapist utilizing exposure therapy will likely do is accompany you to the mall and help you face your fears.

When you are able to see that nothing will happen, anxiety caused by this situation decreases. Again the exposure happens gradually.

The first step might be simply getting in your car and driving to the mall.

Then you might go into the mall for a short period of time.

The next time you might stay a little longer, and so on and so forth.

Now this may sound overly simplistic, but it can be a very effective technique for helping people recover from their anxiety and panic attacks.

Someone not suffering from panic attacks may see this fear as irrational. However, someone who suffers from panic attacks, though, the fear not only seems very real, but it can be very crippling. It's no surprise that sufferers of panic attacks often suffer from agoraphobia.

If you don't know what agoraphobia is, it simply refers to the notion of being scared and avoiding situations that one associates with anxiety and fear. You can see how one might fear going to a mall and instead become accustomed to staying home where they're able to avoid the things that scare them.

The great news is that consistent exposure to these situations that cause intense fear can allow one to confront their fears instead of being controlled by them.

Anxiety cures are available for everyone today, even though they used to be just for a chosen few some years ago there is still hope when you find yourself in the middle of an anxiety attack because it does happen to a majority of people at one point in their lives. It is not true that once you get an anxiety attack you are well on your way to the mental asylum - it takes more than that. Anxiety attacks are caused by several factors, some of which even the medical community is still unaware of.

Before focusing on the right kind of anxiety cures, you have to first differentiate if what you are experiencing is an attack or a full-blown disorder. When you have episodes wherein an overwhelming feeling to run away in fear exists, you can certainly call such episodes anxiety attacks. But you have to remember that it is normal to have these, especially if you are undergoing periods of heavy stressful moments or may have been placed in a situation that you have no control over. On the other hand, when you are having attacks that take place two to four times a day without any reason at all, then you are a candidate for an anxiety disorder.

Anxiety cures can involve Exposure Therapy, where your doctor or therapist helps you figure out the circumstances that cause you to have an attack. Then they will expose you to different kinds of stimuli that will provoke an attack. This is the only way to truly understand your situation, but rest assured you will be under medical supervision at all times. The exposure usually lasts up to twenty minutes per session. After some time, your body learns to respond to the stimuli without feeling overly anxious. After the sessions, you may also be prescribed medications to further help you relax. Since anxiety attacks can also be related to depression, you may also be prescribed anti -depressants that you need to take for a specified period of time.

With the combination of therapy and medication you will be well on your way to living a life free of anxiety.

CONCLUSION

The marrow of cognitive therapy is the hypothesis that unreasoning thoughts and beliefs, overgeneralization of antagonistic events, a hopeless outlook on life, a tendency to focus on problems and failures, and negative self-assessment, as well as other cognitive distortions, further the development of psychological problems, particularly depression. Psychologists use cognitive behavioral therapy to help you identify and understand how these cognitive distortions affect your lifetime.

Most of us think that the situations we encounter and our everyday experiences are the triggers to anxiety, panic and depression. If you are driving your car, for instance, and when you get on a highway you get an anxiety attack, you probably think that your anxiety is caused by driving getting on the highway. This is not true. According to CBT, your thoughts and set of beliefs determines the intensity of your emotions.

Cognitive behavioral therapy gives you simple techniques to stop panic and anxiety attacks dead in their tracks.

CBT is the only method that is able to cure anxiety and panic disorder permanently because it uses scientifically verified strategies to relieve anxiety for a long term. Other popular treatments - like medication, herbal remedies, breathing exercises and more - usually treat anxiety symptoms only and don't treat the root of the problem - Your brain and the way you think!

Although there are pharmaceutical drugs that are used to control anxiety disorders, not all are successful, and many produce unwanted side effects, including neurological damage, impotence, major weaknesses and addiction. There are things you can do to reduce anxiety in a much safer manner.